DUTCH SHEETS *and*
CHRIS JACKSON

SECOND
- in -
COMMAND

Developing Next Generation
Leaders of Excellence

Destiny Image® Publishers, Inc.
P.O. Box 310
Shippensburg, PA 17257-0310

*"Speaking to the Purposes of God for This Generation
and for the Generations to Come"*

ISBN 0-7684-2293-0

For Worldwide Distribution
Printed in the U.S.A.

This book and all other Destiny Image, Revival Press, MercyPlace,
Fresh Bread, Destiny Image Fiction, and Treasure House books are available
at Christian bookstores and distributors worldwide.

1 2 3 4 5 6 7 8 9 10 / 09 08 07 06 05

For a U.S. bookstore nearest you, call
1-800-722-6774.

For more information on foreign distributors, call
717-532-3040.
Or reach us on the Internet:
www.destinyimage.com

ENDORSEMENTS

For the church to succeed we must empower the next generation to reach its fullness in Christ while yet offering a safe environment to grow in. Chris Jackson and Dutch Sheets model the joining of the generations in ministry, lifestyle, and now in this potent book! Filled with wisdom, faith, and transparency, *Second in Command* is a must-read for all emerging leaders!

James W. Goll
Cofounder of Encounters Network
Author of *The Seer, The Lost Art of Intercession,*
and *The Coming Prophetic Revolution*

The quality of a person's life and ministry is often determined by the advisors and confidants he allows to speak into his life. Being second in command is not a statement of importance, but of functional order. Chris and Dutch offer a much-needed discussion on this vital but all too often neglected subject. It would behoove us all to read it and bestow a greater honor to all those called of God to be *Second in Command.*

Norm Willis
Senior Pastor of Christ Church Kirkland
Author, Speaker

It takes a certain "grace" to be second in command. It is not for wimps! Knowing how to navigate safely with the key leader through issues of loyalty amid different vision, trust during life's storms, and honesty in the changing seasons of ministry are a must for Christian servant-leaders today! Paul said, "through love serve one another" (Gal. 5:13). This book helps both support and key leaders know how to work out that love in the ministry among leaders on a day-to-day basis.

Dr. Stan Fleming
Gate Breaker Ministries
Author, Pastor

How encouraging to hear the hearts of a true spiritual son and a true spiritual father! This outstanding book by Pastor Chris Jackson and his spiritual father, Pastor Dutch Sheets, will provide the Body of Christ with insight and encouragement concerning the successful passing of leadership mantles from one generation to the next. Here you will find both principles to learn and warnings that must be overcome in the transfer process. This book underscores the truth: True success in ministry includes succession!

Dr. Jim Hodges
President, Federation of Ministries
and Churches International

This wonderful book breaks the mold. Doesn't everyone want to be "Number One"? Not if God gifts and calls you to be Number Two! Chris Jackson has the realism, the humility, and the personal security needed to be able to explain, clearly and concisely, how his destiny, like John the Baptist's, is to make certain that his leader (Dutch Sheets) flourishes, prospers, and succeeds. I cannot recommend this book enough!

C. Peter Wagner
Chancellor, Wagner Leadership Institute

TABLE OF CONTENTS

INTRODUCTION

It was raining. It was cold. I was beginning to cry. I was 12 years old, and my first day on the paper route had undone me.

I had wanted so badly to prove that I could handle the route. My dad doubted my ability to manage the responsibility at such a young age and it was only with a begrudging consent that he allowed me to take the job at all. He felt that the task would be too overwhelming for a lone 12 year old. He was right.

Just five houses into my route and I was ready to quit. The rain had soaked the newspapers until they unraveled and began to go limp. I was struggling to stay balanced on my bike with their increasing weight.

When I fell, my pants tore and the papers spilled onto the slippery street. I saw blood from a cut on my hand and then I realized that I had lost the route's logbook—I didn't know which way to go next. I crawled to a darkened doorstep, sat down, and wept.

That's when I heard it. A bicycle chain rattled as a large figure loomed into view. It was my father! He had come looking for me in the rain. He had followed me on his own bike and was coasting in to my defeat.

He wasn't angry at me. He just sat down beside me and said, "Why don't we tackle this together?" We found the logbook (about three feet from where I had fallen), and then we gathered the papers, remounted our bikes, and finished the route side-by-side.

At the time I was just glad that he showed up. It wasn't until years later that I began to wonder why he didn't come in our car. The family station wagon was plenty big for a bike and a soaking, 12-year-old boy. Why did he ride his bike in the rain? I think the answer is very simple. I think he was modeling Jesus to me. I think he wanted to meet me right where I was and teach me to succeed in the real world. He was teaching me about true leadership.

Had he tossed me and my wet newspapers in the front seat of our warm car I would have thanked him and then promptly quit the newspaper business. By riding beside me in the pre-dawn fog and teaching me how to throw the papers just right, he instilled courage and tenacity in me. He also set me up for a lucrative career-at least it seemed lucrative to a 12 year old—as a paper delivery boy.

✦✦✦✦✦

What a story! What an experience for a future leader. The man who told it during one of our Sunday morning church services is a seasoned leader with a track record of excellence. His dad imparted something of extreme value to him that day—an understanding that our *heavenly* Father is passionately committed to our victory.

Do you know that to be true? Do you know that God wants to come into your leadership experience and teach you to throw your newspapers just right? He wants to instill courage and tenacity in you. He loves you! He's pedaling toward you right now. He wants you to succeed in your leadership endeavors. That's why I'm writing this book—to strengthen God's leaders.

I am a student of leadership. I love to read leadership books, I love to observe leaders and I love to lead. My goal in this writing, however, is not to simply add another volume to the vast compilation of leadership books that are available today. I'm after a specific niche of leadership. My sights are aimed at the second in command. *I want to strengthen leaders who serve leaders.*

Do you know you're worth your weight in gold? You might not hear that enough so I'd like to say it again. You are needed! You are indispensable to your organization.

You carry the weight of your company as if you owned it. You serve. You support your senior leader. It's far more than a job to you—it's a calling. Some people may not realize the weight that you carry. But I do. I feel like I know you. You're the second in command—and you're worth your weight in gold.

You wouldn't be in your current position unless you were highly motivated and gifted. Although you serve another leader, you, yourself, are a high-level leader. Your hand is on the pulse of your company. You have the ability to wear a dozen hats at once. You could probably run your own organization. In fact, you might some day. You're a blessing.

We need you! Your organization needs you!

In your breast beats a loyal heart. Your senior leader trusts you. Your senior leader leans heavily on you. In fact, you're probably one of his most valuable players. The level of his success will largely be determined by you.

Did I mention that you're worth your weight in gold?

If you do your job well, your entire organization will prosper, your senior leader will look good, and the people you lead will be secure.

You're a leader. But you're a leader who serves another leader.

I'm writing to encourage you.

I'm writing to serve you as you become everything that the Lord has called you to be in your current position.

This book is designed to be a resource for both associate and senior leaders. It will provide a very transparent, in-depth study of both the great challenges and the great rewards associated with the position of the right-hand man or woman. It will serve to encourage and equip associate leaders to handle the unique challenges that are specific to their calling. It will assist them to fulfill Olympic-caliber excellence in that calling while avoiding the pitfalls, snares, and outright demonic attacks that are waged against them. It will also provide senior leaders with a glimpse into the souls of their associates and offer them a fresh understanding of how to minister grace to those they lead.

I want to encourage you and empower you to be a world-class leader in whatever capacity the Lord has called you to. He's proud of you. He loves you. He knows the challenges you face. He's not oblivious to the realities that face the right-hand person. In fact, major portions of the Bible are devoted to the study of assistant leaders.

Joseph was a career right-hand man and yet all of Egypt trembled at his words. Elisha was never known as anything other than the man who "poured water on the hands of Elijah" and yet he performed twice as many miracles as Elijah.

✳ For great churches and businesses to be built in a way that they truly touch the world with the heart of God, there will need to be many men and women who are content to embrace the middle management crunch. Every senior leader needs an army of helpers and an unwavering right-hand man. ✳

Leonard Bernstein was once asked which position in an orchestra was the most difficult to fill. After a moment's reflection he said confidently, "Second fiddle. It's easy to find people who want to play the lead, but to find someone who is content to play second fiddle with excellence and enthusiasm, now that is a rare find."

If you are called as a career right-hand man or woman, I want to serve you in fulfilling your role to the best of your God-given talents and abilities. I want to push you toward a Joseph-like greatness in your calling. God doesn't need you to be in charge to use you greatly.

There are some associate leaders, though, who know that they are ultimately destined to serve in the senior leadership position. They are Joshuas; they have begun as assistants but they know that they are destined to be leaders of mighty organizations.

If you're in a second-in-command position and yet you know that God is grooming you to be the senior leader someday, I want to strengthen you in that process. I want to help you be a Joshua. I want to see the mantle of leadership successfully transferred from your senior leader to you. I hope you go farther than he ever dreamed of going. I hope you represent him well.

Although I am a pastor and I deeply desire to see my fellow pastors blossom as leaders, I'm not writing solely to clergy. I was a businessman before I was a pastor and I am convinced that business is on the mind of God in this hour of history.

In fact, if He is shouting one phrase from Heaven, it is probably the phrase "marketplace ministry." Everywhere I go I hear about it. Every guest speaker who visits our church talks about it. There seems to be a strong consensus that the coming move of God will be, indeed must be, a move of God in the marketplace.

For the full will of God to be done in the earth in this hour, there must be a release of trained and trusted men and women of God into the marketplace. Business leaders must never be overlooked or marginalized. You are crucial for God's agenda to be served in our culture and society!

I'm a pastor in a local church, but you may be a pastor in the marketplace. Whether or not you derive your paycheck from a local church or from the profit of a business, one thing is clear: Leaders are in high demand, and leaders with godly character and excellence are an even rarer find.

Let's be those leaders. Let's grow together through this study of leadership development. Let's be like David who *"served the purpose of God in his own generation"* (Acts 13:36).

So carry on, leader! Your boss needs you. Those you lead need you. The Kingdom of God needs you.

Did I mention that you're worth your weight in gold?

I am more afraid of an army of 100 sheep led by a lion than an army of 100 lions led by a sheep.

-Charles Maurice de Talleyrand-Perigord

A leader is a dealer in hope.

-Napoleon I

People ask the difference between a leader and a boss. The leader leads, and the boss drives.

-Theodore Roosevelt

A leader is best

When people barely know he exists.

Not so good

When people obey and acclaim him.

Worse when they despise him.

But of a good leader

Who talks little

When his work is done,

His aim fulfilled, they will say "We did it ourselves."

-Lao Tse

SECOND IN COMMAND

I never saw it coming. I'm glad it happened, but I was completely unprepared for it. I had planned to soak in the sun and escape from the pressures of college, athletics, and work—I never anticipated a life change. My highest ambition that day was to slowly tan my skin to a deep bronze color—I never expected to encounter my destiny.

It was such a simple question. I'm not sure why she asked it and I still can't believe it changed my life forever. We weren't discussing religion, and God wasn't anywhere near the proximity of my thoughts that day.

I was hurting. My dating relationship with this young woman was rapidly deteriorating. In my first year of college, I was already a hollow man.

I'm so glad she asked the question.

"If you say you're a Christian, why don't you ever talk about God?"

What? What kind of a question was that? Where in the world did that originate? How dare she? Of course I was a Christian! I was saved at five years old. I attended a Christian school for ten years. I had preached in youth groups, my home church, and churches in Mexico a few summers prior. Of course I knew God.

"If you say you're a Christian, why don't you ever talk about God?"

Because, I realized, *I have nothing to say.*

I don't remember if my skin tanned that day. I don't remember exactly when our relationship died. I remember that I encountered Him! A simple question from a young college student had awakened eternity in my soul. If I was, why didn't I?

From that sunburnt moment on I determined that I was, and that for the rest of my life, I would. Thirteen years later, I'm beginning to.

Oh, I've been *talking* about God for a long time, but I'm finally carrying a message from Him. It's been an ugly process to get here. It just about killed me. Perhaps that was His intent all along.

My calling to leadership was awakened that day. Of course it was years before I could be trusted to lead in any significant capacity, but the seed of leadership had finally broken through the soil of my heart and I knew that God had an assignment for me to fulfill. I also knew that I would only find the fulfillment of that assignment in His presence.

For every Christian leader this is the case. I hope you heard me correctly. I said for every *Christian* leader not *church* leader. Christian leaders—in every sector of society—come to life in God's presence. They derive their sense of purpose and significance from Him. They are limited in where they can draw strength and resources. They can't survive long on charisma or personal determination and discipline. They must have *Him.*

Fortune 500 companies can be built on the strength of a man, but the Kingdom of God never can. Fortunes can be won and lost and won again by the guts and tenacity of determined men and women, but to build a lasting legacy of eternal fruit, we must have a divine touch on our lives. To maximize the potential that God has placed within us we must attach the roots of our lives to a source much deeper than our own gifts and talents. We must be cloaked with a grace and anointing that comes from the very breath of God.

The Lord is longing to so cloak us. He places a tremendous value on His leaders. In fact, I think that the words of Malachi are descriptive of His heart for His leaders. He said:

Then those who feared the Lord spoke to one another, and the Lord gave attention and heard it, and the book of remembrance was written before Him for those who fear the Lord and who esteem His name. "And they will be Mine," says the Lord of hosts, "on the day that I prepare My own possession [special treasure]..." (Malachi 3:16-17a).

I realize that this Scripture doesn't specifically address leaders, but it certainly includes them. You need to know that the Lord takes note of your service. He has seen the price that you've paid. He rejoices in your triumphs and He is there to carry you in your defeats. He is not indifferent to the challenges that leaders face. He is especially aware of the challenges that confront associate leaders. I'm aware of them, too.

I am a right-hand man. I serve a great leader. It is an honor to serve him and I deeply appreciate the mentoring that I receive from our relationship. I'm fulfilled in the leadership opportunities that are afforded to me. I'm learning and I'm growing and I want to please the Lord in my service. I want to serve my leader as if he were Jesus. I'm very grateful.

Sometimes, though, I'm miserable. Sometimes the question arises in my heart: "What about me?" You see, although I love my senior leader, I'm called too. I'm trying my best to do a great job as the right-hand man, and yet I have some specific leadership dreams and desires that God has placed in *my* heart too. I deeply desire to obey Jesus' declaration that says that the greatest in the Kingdom of Heaven are those who serve. I *am* a servant and it is indeed an honor to serve; however, I know He has called me to *lead* too.

Does this sound a little too carnal to you? Does it sound self-seeking? Shouldn't I just be happy to serve? Probably. Sometimes I am. But sometimes I'm also ready to lead.

There is a tremendous value within the right-hand man—and, as you well know, there are tremendous challenges that face him. As a leader who serves another leader you need to have great wisdom to navigate the challenges.

What are some of these challenges? Here are a few that you may have experienced.

1.   **You're in charge but you're not in charge.** You're empowered but you don't have the final say. How do you exercise all of your authority while remaining *under* authority?

2.   **You can wonder if your calling is on hold while you serve another man's vision.**

3.   **How do you relate with the senior leader's spouse?** How do the two of you navigate the crossroad of confusion about your roles and responsibilities?

4.   **Sometimes you can be tempted to disloyalty.** How do you effectively lead your team without ever pulling their loyalty away from the senior leader? Those under you can develop utopian feelings about your leadership ability. Some of the most dangerous words that a right-hand man can hear are the words: "If only you were in charge." I'm sure Absalom heard a steady stream of those words before he stole the kingdom from his father, David.

5.   **How do you prepare for the day that you are transitioned into a senior leadership role?** What are the practical steps to ensure that the transition is successful?

6.   **What do you do if you are more gifted than your senior leader?** By the way, if he is a wise leader, he will have staffed his weaknesses with you. Consequently, you *will* be more gifted than he is in certain areas. How then do you maximize your abilities and talents without ever usurping him?

7.   **What if you follow (as in my case) a nationally known leader who carries a great following of respect, love, and admiration?** How do you lead without succumbing to intimidation and fear?

8. How can you carry all of your never-ending responsibilities while still maintaining a commitment to personal growth?

9. How do you relate to visionary leaders?

10. How do you resist the demonic attacks that are leveled at you as the right-hand person?

11. How do you lead and preserve the health of your family?

12. How can you discern the Lord's master plan in the midst of your leadership development?

13. And above all, how can you honor the Lord in your current position? It is in response to these questions that this book is written.

My desire is to wrestle through these issues and answer these questions with you.

I want to offer a quick remark to any female readers. Throughout this book I primarily employ the use of masculine gender pronouns when referencing both senior and associate leaders. This is in no way intended to minimize the incredible value and strength of female leaders. A wonderful aspect of what the Lord is doing in our generation is an honoring and recognition of female leaders. You carry a unique and wonderful aspect of the nature of God that the world can only see *through you*. Your role as a leader should never be marginalized or overlooked!

So let's begin. I think we should start with a little eavesdropping. There is a conversation occurring that contains truth to start us on our journey.

Trust men and they will be true to you; trust them greatly, and they will show themselves great.

-Ralph Waldo Emerson

The only real training for leadership is leadership.

-Anthony Jay

Big jobs usually go to the men who prove their ability to out-grow small ones.

-Ralph Waldo Emerson

WORTH THEIR
WEIGHT IN GOLD

"Why can't the king see it? Why does David still trust him? Joab is a traitor and a murderer!" The young man lowered his voice and continued his tirade more softly to himself: "What a shameful excuse for a leader."

His older companion had been eyeing him carefully as this young, newly promoted soldier railed on the commander of David's army. The young man's outrage was understandable. Just last month, Joab had murdered the king's son. True, Absalom had done the unthinkable. He had betrayed his father, David, and stolen the kingdom from him, but it was still appalling that Joab had killed him in cold blood as he hung from the branches of a tree.

"Joab has done a terrible job leading the army. He is a disgrace to the people of Israel."

The old observer looked at him thoughtfully and interjected gently, "So you were promoted today?"

"Yes. I was commissioned just this morning," the young officer said with a touch of pride.

"Where will you be serving?"

"I have been assigned to serve as the second in command to Abishai, the brother of Joab. I am on my way to consult with him right now."

"What a wonderful opportunity for you," said his friend, with the smile of a pleased father. Then he continued. "I only hope you're half the leader that Joab has been."

Stunned, the young man looked at his mentor with confused and questioning eyes: "*What did you say?*"

"Joab has been one of the greatest leaders of Israel's history. A scrutiny of his life could be one of the most beneficial ways for you to begin your new assignment. Oh, I know that he has betrayed David. Believe me I know. He betrayed him worse than Absalom ever did. Absalom only took the kingdom from David. Joab took his son from him. There's no greater betrayal than what Joab did and surely retribution will some day be served, but what I said is still truth. Joab *is* a world-class leader."

"I've never heard you speak such foolishness. Did you call me here to waste my time with this?"

"I invited you here to share some lessons that will save your leadership career if you heed and apply them. If you would truly serve Abishai and be used of the Lord to strengthen our nation, you must hear me out. Serving leaders is not easy. Indeed, second-in-command leaders, as you referenced yourself, have short life expectancies. They are targeted by the enemy. They are squeezed, sometimes mercilessly, between the senior leader and the people. They carry a tremendous amount of weight and responsibility. Leaders themselves, they must be content to serve. Are you sure you can handle the temptations to power and the fleshly desire to be number one? Are you confident that you can carry your leader's heart in such a way that you please Jehovah Himself? Son, please sit. Hear me out."

"Sir, I am very short on time."

"I will be brief."

The young man sat impatiently as his friend continued.

"Did you know that Joab was one of King David's comrades in the cave of Adullam when he was fleeing from King Saul? I know you would hardly know it today, but there was a time when Joab was a living picture of discouragement and despair. He was one of those distressed, indebted souls who made their way to Adullam when David was a heartbroken fugitive.

"One of the greatest accomplishments that Joab has to his credit is that he survived Adullam. He overcame great personal loss and tragedy to become the chief commander of all the armies of Israel.

"Have you heard how he became the chief of the army?"

"No."

"David had a simple way of identifying leadership among his soldiers. As they faced the enemy host of the Jebusites, David said, 'The first man to strike down and kill a Jebusite will be the commander of the army.' Joab went up first. He struck his man down and returned to the camp as a leader of men.

"Second-in-command leaders must be men of courage and faith. The last thing David needed was a timid man who required constant prodding and coaching and encouragement. He wanted a self-starting warrior of initiative. He found that in Joab."

"That's an interesting way to select a leader."

"Yes, but effective. By using that particular test of leadership, David was ensuring that the new leader would have the respect of the men he would lead. Respect is crucial for success in leadership. Men respect men who lead by example. It's easy to give a command to go fight, but it's an entirely different thing to personally lead your troops into the fray."

"And Joab did that?"

"He still does. He's known for it. He has always personally led his men into battle. Now that he's getting a little older he receives some criticism for it, but he wouldn't have it any other way.

"His presence brings security. His men never wonder where he is because he's right there in front of them. He has bled with them. He has cried with them. He has carried some of them off of the battlefield at risk to his own safety. Some of them have saved his life. They love him."

"That is an admirable quality for a general of his standing."

"It is indeed. And the amazing thing is that he doesn't need to do it anymore. No one would fault him if he stayed behind. Joab is a master strategist. He has pulled off impossible victories and rescues so many times now that he is renowned for his skill in the art and science of war.

"Joab has filled David's leadership role when the king was absent from the army. At the most crucial of moments in a battle, David has often deferred to Joab. He has always trusted that Joab would come through."

"I never said that he wasn't a good general. He has always done well on the battlefield. It's his interactions with David that are so inappropriate."

"What interactions? Do you mean the fact that he confronted David after the death of Absalom?"

"Well, yes, for one. King David was grieving the death of his son—slain by Joab himself—when Joab rebuked him for it. That was the height of insensitivity and arrogance."

"On the contrary, it was the height of sensitivity. Joab wasn't thinking about David at that moment. (You do realize, don't you, that sometimes the needs of the leader must defer to the needs of the people?) David's grief over Absalom was a slap in the face to the men who gave their lives to see his kingdom restored. When David publicly wept for his traitorous son, the glow of victory in his men turned to the pallor of shame and defeat.

"Joab saved David's kingdom that day. He said, in essence, 'You have disgraced yourself and your men by your actions today. If you don't summon your resolve and go bless your people, you'll lose their hearts by nightfall. If this happens, it will be worse than anything that happened to us while we were hunted like dogs at Adullam.'

"That wasn't the only time that Joab confronted David. He was never afraid to risk his own position for the sake of speaking the truth. He was never flippant or casual about it, but he was willing to do it. Sometimes truth needs to be spoken."

"How do you know when to confront your leader? I agree that David risked offending his men, but how do you know when the situation warrants a confrontation?"

"That's a great question, and again, it is Joab who demonstrates the answer. He only confronted David when it was in the best interests of David himself or the people whom David led. He never confronted him over issues of personal opinion and he didn't do it casually as a peer or an equal. He appealed to him. He entreated him. He was always respectful but he did it nevertheless.

"There were several times when Joab appealed to David and was rebuffed. When this occurred, Joab submitted. He was obedient even if he strongly disagreed with the mandate."

"Tell that to Abner! Didn't Joab deceive and murder him in broad daylight immediately after David had made peace with Abner?"

"Yes, Abner was Joab's downfall. Abner had murdered Joab's little brother, Asahel, and Joab could never forget it."

"How then do you say he was a world-class leader?"

"Because his leadership was not defined by a single moment—and neither will yours be. Joab's leadership legacy has been defined throughout a lifetime of faithful service to David.

"He knew David's heart. He deferred to David's leadership. He always sought the best interests of his former cave-dwelling king. When David should have been at war at Rabbah, Joab responded with grace and wisdom. Do you remember the battle at Rabbah? Joab had defeated the army, and the men wanted to place the crown of the vanquished king on Joab's head (his rightful due as the conquering general). Rather than taking the credit for himself, Joab contacted David (who had shamed himself with Bathsheba) and told him to come receive the crown of their enemy.

"This point should be reiterated: Joab knew the strategic moments when David needed to be seen. Joab was fully competent to lead the people and yet he knew when it was appropriate (for both the people and David) for the king to appear on the scene.

"He wasn't in it for personal ambition or glory. I know it appears that he was since he took matters into his own hands on several occasions (like with Absalom and Abner) but he felt that he was doing what was best for David."

At this last statement, the young officer shifted uncomfortably.

"In no way am I condoning any of Joab's actions." The old sage continued quickly. "Joab *is* deceived. As I said a moment ago, I fear that retribution and revenge will come back on Joab's own head before he fulfills his days; however, I do believe that deep within his heart, Joab thinks he is serving the king.

"Deception is deadly. I think the seed of it was sown in him when his brother fell to Abner's spear. Joab never healed and that was his downfall. It's critically important that second-in-command leaders seek for increasing levels of personal growth and healing where needed. Remember, you're a target! An unhealed wound is an entry point for a spirit of betrayal. It got to Joab."

With a gentler expression than he had yet worn in this dialogue, the young commander asked a question. "Are there any other principles that Joab demonstrated that could help me in my relationship with his brother, Abishai?"

The old man smiled. "Yes, there is one more. Joab was an excellent communicator. He faithfully reported every detail of his battles to David. He communicated honestly and thoroughly.

● "Communication is of the utmost importance in your relationship with your leader. As a rule of thumb, *over* communicate. Until he releases you from the need to convey certain details, make it a habit to share everything with him. Joab communicated all relevant details of the activities of the kingdom to David."

"What are relevant details?"

"The senior leader needs to know about anything that could hurt the kingdom. He needs to know anything that people expect him to know. Your leader should never be caught off guard by significant news. Anything that could either significantly hurt (or aid) both the king and his kingdom needs to be communicated immediately. All leadership challenges need to be communicated, too.

"The items that probably do not need to be communicated are distracting trivia. Joab was excellent in discerning, prioritizing, and communicating in all of these areas.

"He did fail in communicating in one crucial area, however. He failed to convey the depth of his personal struggles to David. He never gave David the opportunity to serve *him*. In an attempt to carry the weight of leadership well and to relieve undue stress from David's life, Joab became vulnerable to his own. This cannot be overemphasized: *Do not carry your struggles by yourself.*

"I know you will think that you are serving your leader by hiding your struggles from him. You will be wrong. He needs to know your heart. He can help you. Had Joab expressed the sense of loss and heart-wrenching sorrow that he felt from Abner's murder of his brother, David may have been more thoughtful in his approach to Abner. Had he expressed to David his loathing of Absalom's betrayal, they might have been able to reach a compromise (or David might have sent someone else at the head of his army that day). Absalom may have been imprisoned instead of pierced through with three spears. Joab could have been helped and justified without falling prey to the murderous passions of his heart."

Quite changed over the course of their dialogue, the young officer's face reflected a thoughtful respect. "Thank you," he said softly.

His old mentor responded as he turned to leave, "I think that Abishai has made an excellent choice in you. I believe you will be a great leader who will, indeed, bring increased glory to Israel. I believe in your heart, Son. I believe in your ability. More than that, I believe in *you!*"

The young man was left alone with his thoughts. He wanted to remember these insights. Suddenly, he realized that he knew very little about leadership. He determined at that moment that he would be a leader who served. He would carry the heart of his leader and work to see his leader's vision fulfilled.

Quickly, so he wouldn't forget, he withdrew his commission papers from his satchel, turned them over, and began to write what he had learned on the backside:

1. Second-in-command leaders must be men of courage and faith.

2. They must be self-starting men of initiative.

3. They must earn the trust and carry the heart of their senior leader.

4. They must earn the trust and carry the hearts of those whom they lead.

5. Sometimes they need to speak the truth in love to their leader.

6. They must be excellent communicators, communicating their own personal struggles as well as all pertinent details of the organization.

7. They must be healed of their wounds. Right-hand men are targets of the enemy and unhealed wounds are open doors for the spirit of betrayal.

8. They must be aware of the strategic moments when the senior leader's presence is required.

9. Sometimes their own needs must defer to the needs of the people.

10. They are crucial for the success of the kingdom.

And, lastly, he heard the Lord speak these words into his mind and his spirit: *They are worth their weight in gold!*

Strengthened in his soul, he offered a prayer for Joab and then arose to meet Abishai.

The best executive is the one who has sense enough to pick good men to do what he wants done, and self-restraint enough to keep from meddling with them while they do it.

-Theodore Roosevelt

The challenge of leadership is to be strong, but not rude; be kind, but not weak; be bold, but not bully; be thoughtful, but not lazy; be humble, but not timid; be proud, but not arrogant; have humor, but without folly.

-Jim Rohn

If we were all determined to play the first violin we should never have an ensemble. Therefore, respect every musician in his proper place.

-Robert Schumann

chapter three

NUMBER ONE
IN NUMBER TWO

Do you like *Star Trek*? I don't
think I'm a full-fledged Trekkie,
but I certainly enjoy the show. I
grew up with Kirk, Spock, and McCoy so I admit that I'm a little
partial to the original crew rather than the subsequent spin-offs;
however, I do love *Star Trek: The Next Generation*. I love the cama-
raderie of the crew. I like their psychological—as well as physical—
battles and challenges. I like Captain Picard and Data and Worf, but
I think my favorite character in the *Next Generation* is Commander
Riker, also known as "Number One." Do you like him? I do, but I
feel bad for him.

Although he was called Number One, he was really Number
Two. I think he's just as strong of a leader as Captain Picard. He
could easily command his own starship. I wonder why he isn't ambi-
tious to have his own captain's chair. Why does he settle for being
Number One in Number Two?

Maybe in his mind he isn't settling. Maybe he recognizes the
incredible value of the right-hand man and he knows that not just
anyone can fill that role.

Effective "Number One" leaders have several things in common. Although we learned of several of these in the last chapter, let's review them again:

1. They themselves are gifted leaders.

2. They are skilled communicators.

3. They are alert to the temptation of disloyalty.

4. They carry the heart of their leader.

5. They have a close relationship with their leader.

6. They are servants.

Let's evaluate each of these traits in greater detail.

1. They themselves are gifted leaders.

The right-hand man is both a follower and a leader. Neither of these aspects can be ignored. If I fail to faithfully follow and serve my leader, my own leadership is jeopardized. Likewise, if I do a poor job leading my staff, I fail in my responsibility.

The second in command (the executive officer) is in a unique and challenging position of leadership. They have great trust from those they lead and from those they serve but they also feel great pressure from each of these groups. Sometimes it can feel like you're being torn in two directions. The answer for your approach to each group is the same: *Serve.* To effectively fill your duty as the right-hand man, serve. To efficiently lead your team and gain increasing influence, serve. Servanthood is the key to all successful leadership.

Leadership has been commonly, and accurately, defined as *influence.* The true leader in a given situation is the one who holds the influence in the situation. This leader may or may not be the title holder of the group.

The quickest way to gain influence with those who follow you is to serve them—become one of their biggest fans. Support them. Encourage them. Communicate with them. Spend time with them. Share your heart with them. Pray for them. Believe in them. I once heard someone say, "It's a great thing when the people believe in their leader, but it's an even greater thing when the leader believes in his people." Believe in your people.

Be their cheerleader. Be their coach. Humble yourself when you blow it in communication with them. Ask for forgiveness. Ask for prayer. Lead them even in your failure. Love them.

No amount of vision or charisma will substitute for committed love. If your team knows that they are your number one priority and that you are backing their every step, they will follow you. They will respond when you cast vision. They will contribute when needs arise.

The number two position can really be a fun role to fill. Despite its challenges and frustrations, it contains great authority among your people, along with the security of having help available from above. It's great to know that your leader has your back. (In a later chapter we deal with how to respond if your senior leader fails to provide the oversight and covering that you need.)

Although one of your boss's jobs is to help you when you need it, I suggest that you use him as a last resort. Do as much as you can on your own. Lead as fully as you possibly can. Don't ever make your leader challenge you to step up to the plate, but rather send the message to him that you are striving to carry as much of the weight as possible.

I have made a personal commitment to never back down from intimidating meetings, phone calls, or decisions. I could probably justify passing the buck on some of these; however, I want to be an armor-bearer and a burden-bearer. I never want my leader to feel like he is carrying me. I want him to feel like I am supporting *him.*

Having said this, I must add that wisdom must be liberally applied to this point. If I presume to handle a situation that should have had my leader's input or oversight, I can create a bigger mess than if I had asked for help. I've been guilty of doing this. In attempts to serve and take initiative, I have overstepped my bounds and caused confusion or frustration. When this occurs, the leader needs to step in anyway, so it is much better to gain wisdom in advance and then run with the implementation of it.

2. They are skilled communicators.

Faulty communication has been the bane of many godly organizations. The failure to accurately, frequently, and honestly communicate is one of the quickest ways to deflate morale and derail progress in any organization. I've learned this the hard way. Let me take you into a recent experience.

✦✦✦✦✦

I was shocked! I couldn't believe what I was hearing. After all, *I* was the one who had called the meeting. I was attempting to be a good leader/communicator. Their responses that day changed my leadership philosophy.

It was a special staff meeting that I had called for the purpose of assessing and improving our communication as a team. We were in a season where miscommunication abounded and frustration levels were high. I thought I was being a good leader by taking the bull by the horns and demanding change. Although it *was* positive that I called the meeting, I had no idea that *I* was a major part of the problem.

I had anticipated a positive, healing meeting where I would sit back and help the staff members to resolve their relational and communication differences. As I opened the meeting and began to probe for their honest feelings, however, it became very clear that their frustrations were largely with *me*.

I had become too busy. I had allowed the needs of the members of our church to draw me away from quality time with the staff. Consequently, we weren't communicating as well as we had in the past. Significant decisions weren't being shared with the entire team. Calendar items weren't posted and thoroughly discussed. They were learning about significant decisions when I announced them to the entire congregation from the pulpit. It was wrong, and they were frustrated. I repented and I changed. I had to.

I learned a crucial lesson that day: *A leader's staff must be their top priority.*

3. They are alert to the temptation of disloyalty.

The temptation of disloyalty comes to every right-hand man. The temptation itself has little to do with the character of the right-hand man or their love for their superiors. It just happens. It's one of the many temptations that accompany the number two position. Although we will dissect this dynamic in a later chapter, let me mention that the temptation of disloyalty is spawned from three sources: the devil, hurt or misunderstanding, and disagreements with your leader's decisions.

● *The devil.* Remember that he is trying his best to destroy you. If he can get you to fall, he will have dealt a tragic blow to your organization. He'll try to do this through outright moral temptation or he'll subtly play on your pride and ambition-after all you *are* a highly gifted leader yourself.

● *Hurt or misunderstanding.* You will be misunderstood by your leader at times and you will also misunderstand your leader. The ensuing hurt can set you up for a bout of offense. If this is unchecked, disloyal seeds get sown in your heart and you become a candidate for betrayal.

● *Disagreement with your leader's decisions.* There will be times when you disagree with your leader. Sometimes you will be right. The danger, though, is when you've expressed your views and your leader still insists on pursuing a different course of action. When this happens (and it will) be very mindful of the thoughts that will assault your mind. You'll be tantalized with the message that *you know best.* In some cases, you might. However, those thoughts are precursors to disloyalty. Appeal if necessary. Plead your case. But stay loyal.

4. They carry the heart of their leader.

Without this fundamental character trait, number two leaders are nothing more than liabilities to their senior leaders. A right-hand man with a personal agenda is a deadly thing for a senior leader. A senior leader must know that his number two man understands, respects, and guards his heart and family as if they were his own. The number two man will make or break the senior leader.

John Maxwell, in his book, *The 21 Irrefutable Laws of Leadership*, states that "Every leader's potential is determined by the people closest to him." With this being true, it is impossible to divorce the success of the organization from the contribution of the second-in-command leader.

There will be many times in the daily administration of his duties when the right-hand man must make decisions based on what he thinks the senior leader would want. In my position I am not only responsible for the specific areas under my supervision, but I am also responsible for administrating the big picture vision of our church. I am empowered to make many decisions that I feel would best serve the ministry. To ensure that my decisions are correct, I must be very careful to factor in the heart of my leader to those decisions that affect the overall health and direction of our church.

The desires of the senior leader's heart are priority for the organization. I have a lot of dreams that I want to see fulfilled in our church, but the primary vision comes from our senior leader. He carries the vision. I carry his heart.

5. They have a close relationship with their leader.

I don't need to be best friends with my leader. I've never thought that God called me here to hang out with my boss; however, we do need to have a close relationship. If I don't know him, how can I know his heart? If he doesn't know me, how can he care for me as my leader?

Let me offer a few suggestions on relating and socializing with your senior leader.

Relate on his terms. Remember, you're there for him, not vice versa. My boss likes the Denver Broncos. I like boxing. Do you know what we do when we hang out together? We watch the Broncos. And I love it. I'm still a boxing fan but my God-assigned responsibility is to serve him and help him carry the weight of the vision.

Sometimes there's nothing more refreshing than relaxing and playing with our leaders and our coworkers. We spend a lot of time together putting out fires and strategizing and dealing with problems.

It's nice to laugh together. I want to be a source of refreshing for my boss. I just hope he doesn't ask me to start hunting with him.

Allow the fun times to truly be fun. During the halftime of a Broncos game is not the appropriate setting to ask his opinion on the latest pressing issues. It's very easy to allow the pressing needs of your business to permeate every conversation, but it's not always appropriate or healthy. I have to work at this. If I'm not careful, I'll find myself mentioning details about one of our church's ministries or asking a question about a pending need or opportunity. Sometimes we just need to be *people,* not leaders. Sometimes we need to play, not work.

Recently, he came into my office and said, "Gather all of the staff guys—tell them we're going skiing tomorrow." What a day it was! Colorado is famous for its brilliant blue skies, champagne snow, and world-renowned ski resorts. We had the time of our lives. One day of playing as a team bonded us more than all of the prior year's staff meetings.

Take the initiative. Don't make him carry you—even regarding fun. If you can see he has been under a lot of pressure, take the initiative to either do something fun together or arrange things so he can get away with his wife for a night. You probably have a good sense for what situations must be handled personally by the senior leader. Sometimes it is very appropriate for you to tell him to skip a certain meeting or postpone a particular activity if he needs the rest. I'm constantly trying to take the weight of pressure and responsibility off my leader's shoulders. Sometimes I'll assure him that I can step up to the plate to handle a particular situation so he can have an evening with his family.

Follow his lead. The right-hand man must wear multiple hats in his relationship with the senior leader. Sometimes we are peers as we strategize about vision and direction for our church. At other times, we are merely friends eating lunch together. There are other times, though, when he needs to be the leader. Although I, too, am a leader, he's the man.

It's important to carefully assess when the hats need to change. Sometimes your leader will want a friend or an encourager. Don't be afraid to step into that role. Regardless of the situation, however, respect must be a constant. Even on the ski slopes when he feels his age, I must never cross the lines of respect and courtesy.

Realize that he will need some peer level friendships. No matter how close you get or how deeply into his confidence he pulls you, there will be times when he will need to speak with someone on a peer level. You should never be intimidated or insecure about this. It's very healthy for your leader to relate to other leaders of equal or greater influence.

Take an interest in his family. His family is the dearest thing in his heart. The quickest way to gain his loyalty and trust is to serve his family. Go out of your way to bless and serve his spouse and children. Remember their birthdays and special events. Many people will take their shots at him and his family. You have his back.

6. They are servants.

Before Jessica and I moved to Colorado Springs to assume the position of second in command in our current church, I made appointments with my senior pastor and his executive pastor. Since I would be serving as an executive pastor I wanted to glean some wisdom from each of them that would help to ensure a successful tenure in this position.

I met with each pastor separately and asked them the same question: "What are the best ways that I can strengthen my senior leader?" Their responses were wonderfully helpful and surprisingly similar.

My senior pastor listed the following as his top suggestions:

1. Make frequent phone calls asking the question "Is there anything you need?" It is one thing to do a good job with the leader's requests but it is an entirely different and better thing to instigate the request.

2. Be available to spend time together—lunches and dinners—as needed.

3. Respond in faith to spiritual warfare, crises, or challenges. If the team is faced with a problem, the right-hand man should be the first to run to the battlefield.

4. Do their tasks right away. If the senior leader asks for a particular task to be done, it should immediately go to the top of the list. Your senior leader should know that if he assigns it to you, it's done.

When I spoke with the executive pastor, his responses were as follows:

1. Check in both before and after key meetings. Be available.

2. Always bring encouragement before every church service. Never let the service begin without providing some form of support. From complimenting his tie to urging him to preach with boldness, do something to let him know that you believe he will do a great job in the service.

3. Always keep an eye on his children. If your senior leader has children, make a conscious effort to reach out to them in love and encouragement. If appropriate, spend time with them. Let him know that you are as protective of them as you are of him.

4. Help with practical needs. Sometimes just handling an oil change in a vehicle can alleviate tremendous stress in a hectic week.

5. Guard against pride when a deep, relational connection grows. You will be brought into special confidences—don't allow this to become a source of pride.

6. Become a Denver Broncos fan (or at least be willing to enjoy a game).

7. Wear bifocals. In other words, keep your eyes on both the big picture as well as the details. Even as you strive to faithfully implement the vision, learn what little things concern him and keep them shored up and tidy.

What would Captain Kirk have been without Spock? What would Picard have been without Number One? Your leader needs you.

Second in command is not an easy role to fill. Learning to be Number One in Number Two can be very challenging. Some of the greatest challenges come in the form of questions. "What about me? Am I not called, too? Is my vision on hold while I serve the vision of another?"

In the next chapter, let's explore these questions and glean some insights that will help us safely navigate them.

A man who wants to lead the orchestra must turn his back on the crowd.

-Max Lucado

In order to become a leading home run hitter, a batter must be surrounded by good hitters; otherwise, the pitchers will "pitch around" him. Likewise, many successful people became that way from being on a good team.

-Laing Burns Jr.

When the great Polish pianist Ignacy Jan Paderewski was elected prime minister of his country, he made one request before accepting the prestigious office. He would lead the country, but he must be allowed to practice his scales for two hours every day. Guitar virtuoso Andres Segovia requires the same of his students—two hours a day of playing scales. Yet who plays scales in a concert?

It is the mastery of the basics that gives birth to freedom of expression, ease of movement, and cohesiveness in the delivery of each phrase.

-Wayne Cordeiro

BUT I'M CALLED, TOO!

The emotion was nearly unbearable. He could scarcely control the tremor in his voice. Although he stood face-to-face with Jesus Himself, his heart was still broken into a thousand shards of pain. He wanted to run. He wanted Jesus to gather him into His forgiving arms. He didn't deserve to be here. He should still be fishing at sea.

"What is that to you, Peter? You follow Me." The words cut through the fog of Peter's grieving mind and pierced his heart with fresh hope. Jesus spoke again, "If I want John to remain until I come, what is that to you? That doesn't affect your place at My side at all. Your destiny is to follow Me. No one else can take your place. I didn't need two Johns. John's place with Me is secure *and so is yours.* I need you. Now, follow Me!"

For the first time in days the crushing weight of guilt seemed to roll off Peter's shoulders and slip, forgotten, into the sea. Gentle wavelets lapped the shore of Galilee and erased the failure of the past weekend. With each cry of the gulls a new cry of hope arose in Peter's soul. Perhaps he really could be forgiven. Perhaps the Lord really did see something in him that superseded his failure. It hardly seemed possible. He had been as much of a traitor as Judas.

A few days earlier, Judas had hung himself in shame. Peter had run away. He denied ever knowing the carpenter from Nazareth.

Then, when he should have comforted and strengthened the remaining disciples, he convinced them to go back to their past with him. Sadly, he couldn't even fish anymore. With each empty cast of his nets his heart broke a little more. As his fingers grew numb in the midnight cold, an icy grief encased his soul in regret. Why had he denied Him? Why didn't he have the courage to stand with Him in His darkest hour?

His boastful words still shamed his heart as they echoed in his ears: "Though everyone else denies You, *I* will never deny You." He remembered John's expression when he had said those arrogant words. John had looked thoughtfully at Peter and bowed his head in silence. John was the only one who stood at Jesus' side at Calvary. He held Mary in a crushing embrace as she wept from the depths of her soul. Jesus had even spoken to him: "Son, behold your mother."

Peter had seen Jesus since His resurrection. He and John had raced to the empty tomb and confirmed the women's story. He had risen like they said. He really was the Messiah. However, as awesome as it was, the elation of seeing Him alive had not yet healed the sense of failure and regret.

They hadn't spoken yet.

Peter had worshiped at Jesus' feet. He had wept and embraced Him but they hadn't spoken about *it* yet. So he sat on the bottom of the boat in mournful silence.

They had been fishing all night and the depression was choking Peter. Although the sun was rising and its radiant glory was reflected in the early morning waves, Peter was about to break again when he heard the voice.

"Cast your nets on the other side of the boat!" Instinctively, they obeyed. What ensued was a euphoric sense of nostalgia mixed with elation and the scent of new beginnings. Their nets were so full of fish that they could barely lift them out of the water.

Peter remembered his first encounter with the Lord when his nets broke under the weight of the blessing. At that time, he had fallen at Jesus' feet and begged for mercy. "Depart from me for I am a sinful man, Lord." The Lord's response was engraved forever in Peter's memory. "Follow Me, Peter. From now on you will catch men."

The memories washed his soul with a mixture of fear and hope as they toiled to haul in the nets. Would Jesus be merciful once again or would He be angry for Peter's denial and subsequent return to the past?

He worked until he couldn't take it any longer. He jumped to his feet and hurled himself overboard, swimming toward the shore in a frantic attempt to get to Jesus' side. When he arrived, however, the fear so assailed him that he again avoided the inevitable eye contact. Instead, he began counting the catch of fish.

"One hundred and fifty-two, one hundred and fifty-three..." Jesus interrupted, "Boys, do you have any breakfast?"

They ate in silence and a surreal peace settled over their anxious hearts. Jesus didn't seem angry. He kept looking deeply into their eyes. What they saw there was an endless supply of understanding and love.

Finally, He spoke to Peter, "Let's go for a walk."

The restoration was wonderful. Sure, it hurt a little, as it always does to repent, but Peter was set free. He confronted his failure. He acknowledged the frailty of his own soul. Then he was called again. "Feed My sheep!" The joy that erupted in Peter's soul spread as a grin across his tear-stained face. Again, "Feed My lambs."

As they walked along the beach, Peter heard a scuffling sound behind them. He turned to see John following them. A momentary wave of fear passed over him again. "Lord, what about this man?" That's when He said it.

"If I want him to remain until I come, what is that to you? My plan for his life has zero effect on yours. Peter, I've called you to follow Me. I love John. He will always have a place against My chest and He will always hear the sound of My heartbeat, but that shouldn't threaten you. I didn't need two Johns. Yes, I need him and he will reveal a part of My nature to the churches, but I also need you. I need a rock that I can build upon. That's *you*, Peter! Don't ever allow comparison or insecurity to enter your thinking. I need you! But I need you to be all of you. Anytime our enemy assails your mind with fear and self-doubt, just remember My command: Follow Me. I ordained you to be with Me. Your security stems from that place.

"If I want him to remain until I return, what is that to you? *You follow Me!*"

✦✦✦✦✦

Have you ever been Peter? Have you ever felt threatened by your own failure or by someone else's success? Don't feel guilty if you have. I follow a nationally known leader who is renowned for his ability to expound and preach the Word of God. Sometimes I doubt my ability to fill his shoes.

That's when the Lord reminds me: "I didn't call you to fill his shoes. I called you to be *you*. You're not in competition with your senior leader and nor is he with you. I needed you both and I will use you both. If I choose to give him favor in certain circles and bear My name on an international platform, what is that to you? You follow Me."

Associate leaders who feel called to serve in senior leadership roles can be especially vulnerable to this struggle. They can begin to doubt if they are really fulfilling their calling in their current position.

Whether or not you feel called to serve the Lord in a senior leadership role, you must still resolve the questions of "What about me?" and "Am I not called too?"

So what about those questions? Aren't you called, too? It's not just your senior leader who has a mandate from the Lord to fulfill. What about you? Is your calling on hold while you serve another man's vision?

The answer is both "yes" and "no."

Yes, certain aspects of your personal vision and life mission are on hold while you serve someone else, but, no, you don't have to lay down your dreams while you help make another man's dreams come true.

Let's discuss several responses to this thought.

First, you will always serve someone else's vision. Jesus did. He never did anything that His Father did not initiate. He was the ultimate servant of another's vision.

Second, serving someone else's vision is a prerequisite for being entrusted with your own. The more diligently you serve someone else's vision, the more quickly the Lord opens doors for you to pursue your own vision.

Third, loyalty to your leader's vision will be reciprocated. The more faithful you are to serve your leader's vision, the more sensitive he will be to allow opportunities for you to pursue yours.

Fourth, the Lord usually gives you Leah before He gives you Rachel.

Fifth, Rachel's release is determined by Leah's embrace.

To understand these last two points, we must review a familiar Bible story. It is found in Genesis 29 and you can study it in its entirety there. For now, I'm simply going to analyze one particular aspect of the story.

◆◆◆◆◆

It is Jacob's wedding day. He's waited seven years for this moment. He has wanted to marry Rachel since the first moment he saw her. When she first spoke to him, his heart found its home. She was gorgeous. She was virtuous. She was his.

Her father wasn't convinced, however. He made Jacob work for seven years to prove his worth before he would consent to their marriage. Despite the severity of the requirement, Jacob submitted and worked with a vision of her loveliness held ever before his heart.

Surprisingly, the time passed quickly. His love for her so overshadowed his world that he passed through his seven years of toil as if they were seven days. Indeed, he would have worked a lifetime for her hand.

When the day came and Rachel was finally his, he knew that every moment of toil was worth it. They were wed. Life made sense.

The lights were extinguished and he entered her tent.

The next morning was the darkest day of Jacob's world.

Rachel had an older sister who was unmarried, and her father didn't want her to experience the shame of seeing her little sister wed first, so he did the unthinkable. He swindled Jacob. He betrayed him. He broke him. He replaced Rachel with Leah.

When the time came for Jacob to enter Rachel's tent, he didn't know that Rachel had actually been replaced by her older sister. Leah lay quietly in the dark waiting for her sister's groom. Rachel wept in her father's tent.

In the morning, Jacob's world caved in. The woman in his arms was not Rachel.

Rachel was beautiful; whereas Leah, the Bible says, was "tender-eyed," which meant "tired- or weak-eyed."

Jacob loved Rachel. The Bible says that he hated Leah.

Two weeks later, Rachel's father allowed Jacob to marry Rachel as well. There was just one slight catch. In addition to keeping Leah, Jacob was also sentenced to seven more years of service. He had two wives. He was trapped at his father-in-law's home. His vision of Rachel had faded into Leah. And then he got more bad news.

Rachel was barren.

Jacob's vision of loveliness was replaced with a reality of barrenness. His dreams crumbled for the second time. He cried. He cursed. He pleaded with God. And then he discovered something else.

Leah was incredibly fertile. In fact, it seemed like every time he embraced her she conceived.

He loved Rachel. The vision for his life was wrapped up in Rachel. What he had been given though was Leah, and she looked nothing like the dream that he had been carrying in his heart.

Jacob was experiencing a powerful principle that every emerging young leader must learn. *The Lord gives you Leah before He gives you Rachel. And, Rachel's release is determined by Leah's embrace.*

There were some elements of Jacob's life that only Leah could give him. Every time he embraced Leah (despite his disappointment), life was released. Gifts were added to him. An inheritance, sons, was begun.

The Lord wants to know if you will embrace Leah. He has called you to Rachel, but your Leah will add some things to your character and leadership ability that Rachel can't give you—at least not initially.

Rachel did, eventually, conceive and bear a son to Jacob. However, it didn't happen until Jacob had faithfully embraced Leah.

Leah bore him Reuben, Simeon, Levi, and Judah. Their names meant *seeing, hearing, attachment,* and *praise,* respectively. When Jacob embraced Leah, God gave him the ability to truly see and hear. When he embraced her again, he received a stronger attachment to the purposes of God. When he embraced her, yet again, he truly learned the power of praise.

Jacob needed Leah.

And so do you. And so do I.

Do you feel like you're being asked to embrace Leah? It's okay if you do. It's not disrespectful toward your leaders if you feel that your current assignment is a Leah. God knows what He is doing. Just embrace her as you remind Him that what you signed up for was Rachel.

He holds back Rachel until we are content with Leah. Our destiny, like Jacob's, is to be transformed into princes of God. Princes require a lot of grooming and preparation before they're ready for the throne. Sometimes that preparation comes in the form of a strange woman hiding in a tent.

Embrace her. She has life to give you. You'll need every gift she provides when you finally get to Rachel.

Oh, yes, you'll eventually get to embrace Rachel. She eventually gave birth to a son. Often, though, her release is contingent on your embrace of her sister.

The sweet irony of Jacob's story is seen at the end of his life when he charges his sons with his burial requests. On his death bed, he made a specific request of his sons. He said, "Bury me at Machpelah in Mamre where Abraham buried Sarah [the love of his life] and where Isaac buried Rebekah [the love of his life], *and where I buried Leah.*"

Jacob fell in love with Leah.

You *are* destined for the Rachel that you fell in love with when you responded to the leadership call on your life. You must remember, though: *Leah is part of Rachel.* You need both.

God gives us Leah before He gives us Rachel. Rachel's release is often determined by Leah's embrace.

You might be the second in command, but aren't you called too? Of course you are! Be encouraged. The preparation you are enduring is testimony to the greatness of your calling.

You're called to be a prince.

No man is fit to command another that cannot command himself.

-William Penn

We are what we repeatedly do. Excellence then, is not an act, but a habit.

-Aristotle

First we form habits, and then they form us. Conquer your habits or they will conquer you.

-Ron Gilbert

Men acquire a particular quality by constantly acting in a particular way.

-Anonymous

How use doth breed a habit in a man!

-William Shakespeare

THE WAY OF THE LEADER

The Olympics. Don't you love them? Aren't they awesome to watch? They inspire me!

I love to watch Olympians compete in the Olympic Games. I love to watch world records fall. I love to watch the gymnasts leap and flip and spin and twist and stick their landings. I love to watch champions emerge. I love to watch an unknown kid from another part of the world set a new record and become a household name.

I love the stories of the athletes' discipline and devotion. I get inspired when I hear about their commitment levels and their devotion to their dreams. It's fun to watch them win. It's sad to watch them fail.

I like to know the personal side of the games. I'm always stirred by their stories of triumph and tragedy. Sometimes I'm moved to tears by the adversity that different ones have overcome.

Jessica and I clear out our schedule every two years to do nothing but cuddle up and watch the Games. We love the Olympics.

I think I've figured out why they affect me so deeply. I used to think it was simply the excellence of the competition and the glory that is seen in the gathering of the nations, but there's actually another reason. The New Testament makes it very clear that followers of Jesus Christ are called to function with Olympic-caliber excellence in whatever they do.

This is especially true of leaders.

When the apostle Paul wrote his letters to the Corinthian believers, he was writing to a group of people who had a similar love for the Olympics. The biennial Olympic Games originated in Corinth and were a significant part of the city's culture. When Paul addressed the church there he used Olympic terminology. Listen to some of the phrases he used in First Corinthians 9.

> *Do you not know that those who run in a race all run, but only one receives the prize? Run in such a way that you may win* (1 Corinthians 9:24).

Win means to catch or to seize. It literally means to come from behind to capture the victory. It reminds me of one of the recent swimming matches in the 2004 Olympics in Athens, Greece, when Michael Phelps came from behind to out-touch Crocker for victory at the wall.

> *Everyone who competes* [agonizomai] *in the games exercises self-control in all things. They then do it to receive a perishable wreath, but we an imperishable* (1 Corinthians 9:25).

Competes, from the Greek word *agonizomai,* is truly an Olympic word. It literally means to contend for victory in the public games. Agonizomai. If you read it out loud, you can hear the English word *agony* in it. It reminds me of the old Wide World of Sports program that began each episode with the phrase "the thrill of victory and the agony of defeat." The word also means "to strain every nerve to the uttermost in contention for victory." That's certainly descriptive of Olympic athletes.

They push their bodies to the breaking point-some literally collapsing at the end of a race or a swim or a routine. Agonizomai originates from the Greek verb *Ago,* which means to toil with force or violence. Some lexicons and study aids even reference the Olympic sports of running, boxing, and wrestling to describe the type of intense competition inherent in the word. Paul said the Olympians did it to receive a laurel wreath that wilts (or, nowadays, a gold-plated medal that will hang on a wall). We do it, he said, for a wreath imperishable.

Did you know that you're in the Olympics? Every Christian is, although many don't realize it.

The author of Hebrews uses similar terminology when he says: *"Therefore, since we have so great a cloud of witnesses surrounding us, let us also lay aside every encumbrance and the sin which so easily entangles us, and let us run with endurance the race that is set before us"* (Heb. 12:1).

He goes on to say: *"You have not yet resisted to the point of shedding blood in your striving against sin"* (Heb. 12:4). The term *striving against* is our term for agonizomai. He said that we should approach our fight against sin with the same tenacity with which an Olympic wrestler faces his opponent. We should be straining every nerve to the uttermost in our contention for victory over the enemy of our soul.

By the way, *our enemy* is attacking us with Olympic-caliber force. In Ephesians 6:12, Paul says that *"Our struggle [agonizomai] is not against flesh and blood, but against the rulers, against the powers, against the world forces of this darkness, against the spiritual forces of wickedness in the heavenly places."* Like it or not, believe it or not, agree with it or not, we are in a war of Olympic proportions.

What a ludicrous proposition it would be to think that a weekend warrior (like me) who exercises a couple of times a week could compete against an Olympic athlete. I like to lift weights and run on a treadmill for about 30 minutes, a few times each week. What a joke to think that I could win the gold in Beijing in 2008. How crazy to think that I could last even a few seconds with the greatest wrestlers in the world.

But that's what we do spiritually.

We live on a few minutes of daily devotions and hope to withstand an enemy who is devoted to our destruction with Olympic-level intensity. Not only is he devoted to the downfall of individuals, but he is especially intent on destroying godly businesses and ministries. If he can stop an individual, he is pleased; but if he can stop a leader, he rejoices. Leaders influence people. Leaders are a threat to the kingdom of darkness.

Leaders are bigger targets.

What can we learn from the Olympics that can serve to enhance our leadership ability and ensure our success? All Olympians have one thing in common. Despite their different life experiences and ethnic backgrounds and personal struggles, they all possess one common denominator: *They live a lifestyle that supports their ambition.* They don't just train really hard a few months during the off-season. Their lives revolve around the pursuit of their dreams.

There was a young girl from Washington State (my home state) who competed in swimming in the 2000 Sydney games. Her life didn't look the same as every other 16 year old in her high school. She was in the pool every morning at 4:00 A.M. After school, she practiced for three more hours. She only ate foods conducive to improving her strength and stamina. She had to go bed early. She surrendered her freedom out of devotion for her dream.

Although most Olympic athletes may not realize it, they are actually practicing a very biblical principle. They are living *the way*. The Hebrew word *Derek* (translated "way") is used all throughout the Old Testament. It is an incredibly powerful word that refers to a way, mode, or manner of living. It refers to the way in which one takes a journey or approaches a task. It means *lifestyle*.

In the Hebrew mind there was no compartmentalization of religion. People were their beliefs. They lived the way of devout ones. In the Book of Proverbs, King Solomon urged a young man to keep his *way* pure. He didn't say "avoid lust and immorality"; he said "keep your entire lifestyle far from the adulterous woman."

It's interesting that the early disciples of Jesus Christ were called members of *The Way*. They lived a lifestyle of devotion to a cause. Just like Olympians do.

Just like we should.

Success in any endeavor comes from creating a way of living that sustains victory and success. Success is never the result of mere inspiration. I can get inspired very easily; however, great works aren't accomplished by bursts of brilliant inspiration. People have these bursts every New Year, but the reason that most New Year's resolutions fail is because those making the resolutions fail to create a lifestyle that sustains their new resolve. They are very genuine in their desire to change, but they don't move beyond desire into action. They don't sculpt a new way of living.

What is the way of the leader? How can we craft a lifestyle that ensures success in our leadership callings?

I think the answer is twofold:

1.   Identify priorities.

2.   Create a system that supports and sustains them.

Identifying priorities is crucial for any leader. There is always more work than a leader can get done in a given day. I'm sure your to-do list is never fully deleted. There is always one more sales call to be made. There's always one more client to see. The leaders who practice the discipline of identifying priorities (and living within them) are the leaders who accomplish the most in life and have the most time left over for alternate pursuits of happiness.

I was privileged to eat lunch with a great man of God when I was just starting out in my leadership career. He was a guest speaker at our Bible college, and it was a tremendous honor to receive a few minutes of his time. Several young adult leaders had been invited to this luncheon, and as we joked and small-talked, he said, "Let's redeem the time. Is there anything on your hearts today that I can address?"

He was a renowned author and speaker with a busy schedule that led him into dozens of nations annually. He had a precious wife and several small children and he also held the position of senior pastor of his church—a thriving congregation in a busy, metropolitan city. I asked my question: "How do you do it? How do you accomplish all that you do and still maintain your family priorities?"

His response was swift and sweet and it marked my life forever. He quoted the apostle Paul who said in Second Corinthians 10:13-14: "*We will not boast beyond our measure...we are not overextending ourselves....*" He explained to us that the word *measure* was the Greek word *metron*, and it referenced the metered-out space that the Lord has assigned for every leader. He emphasized the fact that there are a lot of things a leader can do, but he is only called to do those things that fall within his God-assigned measure.

Stay within your measure! It's there that your anointing flows best. It's there that you will have the greatest influence and impact. It's there that you will change the world.

Defining your measure makes your life much easier. If you know, specifically, what the Lord has called you to, you can say no to everything else. This is both freeing and redemptive.

How does the second-in-command leader determine his measure?

First, he doesn't determine it alone. We need to get input from the senior leader. There is a vantage point that the senior leader has that other leaders are not graced with. There have been occasions when I was certain that I should direct the bulk of my time in a particular area but later realized, through counsel with my senior leader, that I would add more value to our organization if I went in a different direction.

Where should you focus your energy? I heard John Maxwell say to a group of leaders, "You are most valuable where you add the most value." Where do *you* add the most value? You probably know the answer, but your leader probably has some additional insight.

As a general rule of thumb for determining your measure, follow these principles:

1. *Do what God has called you to do.* You will be the most anointed, effective, and fulfilled in this area.

2. *Serve your senior leader.* Someone said, "The senior leader serves the people; the staff serves the senior leader." There's truth in that statement.

3. *Focus on the specific strengths that you alone bring to your organization.* Since you are a high level leader, you are probably privileged with the ability and freedom to staff your weaknesses. Do it. Don't waste a lot of time trying to become excellent in your weak areas, but rather strive to master and maximize your strengths.

I have identified my measure (in my position of church leadership) to include the following:

1. Seeking the will and presence of God for my church.

2. Serving my senior pastor. His requests must be top priority.

3. Communicating (teaching and preaching) in corporate settings.

4. Pastoring my staff. I must prioritize those leaders that I lead.

5. Providing pastoral care for our congregation.

When I get out of my measure I immediately lose my effectiveness as a leader. For example, if I devote the bulk of my time to the needs of the people in my congregation, my staff and ministry leaders feel neglected. This is dangerous because *they* are the ones who are truly pastoring the people. If I am a wise leader I will invest my time with them to ensure that my pastoral efforts are multiplied. I can provide much more effective leadership and pastoral care for the congregation by investing the bulk of my time into my leaders.

I know this sounds very simplistic and obvious, yet many leaders fail here. Especially church leaders.

Most church leaders were trained in a Bible college and, while they learned the ins-and-outs of sermon preparation and spiritual development, they learned very little about leadership. Consequently, many pastors are playing catch up. They are wonderful pastors (in the true, shepherding sense of the word), yet they struggle in the area of leadership. I do too. Sometimes I forget that I can get more done by ministering to a few key leaders than I can by personally visiting with 40 people from our church each week. Of course the prioritization of my leaders does not negate my need to be available for the members of the congregation—it actually enhances it.

Let's go back to systems. I mentioned that the reason that most resolutions fail is that they are never sustained by a *system* that ensures success. Creating a system does not have to be a complicated affair. Once I identified my ministry priorities, I simply looked at the amount of hours that were available to me for work (I began the process by reserving plenty of time to be with the Lord and my family) and I began assigning time to my priorities.

We all have the same amount of time allotted to us each week. The choice is ours how we use it. I have realized that my mornings are the most productive time of the day for me; therefore, I reserve them for my priorities. I have to be very intentional about this.

It's easy to enter my office and check my Emails first. When I do this, I have usually lost an hour of time and become bogged down by the content of varying correspondences. Before I know it, I've lost my prime *priority time* and then my day's appointments are upon me.

Create a system. I learned and practiced this principle when I was the right-hand man in a start-up mortgage company, and it worked wonders for us. We increased our bottom line and we received greater appreciation and referrals from our customers.

As a new, unknown company in a city dominated by well-established banking institutions, my partner and I realized that we needed an edge to help us succeed. Since interest rates were at a 40-year low, all of the city's mortgage companies were aggressively pursuing the refinance market. We, of course, wanted a piece of that market, too, but we realized that our odds of competing with some of the existing companies were quite slim.

After much prayer and strategy, we felt like the Lord was inspiring us to develop a very simple (yet excellent) servicing system for real estate agents. No Realtors would refer business to us based on the strength of our name (they didn't know our name). So we surmised that our best edge was to provide the most excellent and innovative customer service plan in the industry.

I know that sounds lofty and I doubt if we accomplished that goal; however, we did gain favor with numerous Realtors who had never experienced that type of follow-up and care for their referred leads and customers. We took the concepts of gratitude, servanthood, and faithfulness and built them into a system that included daily updates and referral gifts, as well as *marketing opportunities.*

We asked the questions: "How can we serve our Realtors? How could *we* refer business to *them*?" Once we identified several simple but effective ways, we built the system. The system told me on what day to send the thank-you cards. It told me how often to contact them with updates. It ran that particular aspect of our company for me. All I had to do was run the system.

We were greatly inspired by a book called *The E-Myth* by Michael Gerber. In it, he demonstrated how the most successful corporations are those that develop a turn-key system of operation. If a system is put in place that efficiently runs the company, all the employees have to do is work the system. If there is no system, the people might still be able to get the work done, but the effort required to accomplish it increases dramatically.

Every business needs a system of operation to survive. Every New Year's resolution needs a system to sustain it and ensure its implementation. It's the way of the leader.

The Power of an Hour

Before I conclude this chapter, I'd like to share an amusing discovery I made one day while I was pondering all of the things that I wanted to accomplish with my life and yet felt the pressure of having too little time. I decided to examine what I could accomplish if I devoted just 95 minutes each day to my priorities. Glance at the following chart to see what I discovered.

The power of daily discipline continued over time:

95 minutes/day for 3 years

95 minutes/day for 25 years

Activity	Time (per day)	3-Year Results	25-Year Results
Prayer	30 minutes	3.5 months of 40-hour work weeks of intercession	2.25 years of 40-hour work weeks of intercession
Bible reading (with a simple Bible reading schedule)	20 minutes	Old Testament 3X New Testament 6X Psalms and Proverbs 6X	Old Testament 25X New Testament 50X Psalms and Proverbs 50X
Writing	15 minutes	1 book published	8 books published
Reading	15 minutes	22 books total: 9 spiritual books 9 biographies 4 novels	182 books
Exercise	15 minutes	273 hours	2,281 hours = enough energy and strength to keep up with my grandkids

Remember, the Creation story began with God telling time what to do and how to be labeled. He said to it: "Evening, Morning, you'll be one day. This is how you will function." We're called to do the same.

The primary keys to living the way of the leader are to:

1. Identify your priorities and stay within that measure.

2. Create a system that supports the priorities of your measure.

3. Tell time where to go.

4. Then, go change the world!

The first responsibility of a leader is to define reality. The last is to say "thank you." In between, the leader is a servant.

-Max DuPree

There are only three kinds of people: those who are immovable, those are movable, and those who move them.

-Li Hung Chang

The story is told of two prisoners lying on their bunks one evening. The prisoner on the top bunk was staring out the window of his cell into the night sky. The stars were spread out in a splendid array, with an occasional shooting star making the evening sky a spectacular display of divine fireworks.

Calling to his cell mate in the bunk below, the man said, "Hey, wake up! Look at the stars! They're beautiful. Look!"

"Aw, leave me alone," his cell mate grunted.

"Come on. Just look. The stars tonight are the brightest I've ever seen."

His cell mate groaned and turned over in his bunk to look out at the night sky. After a brief glance, he growled, "I don't see any stars. All I see are bars."

One prisoner saw the stars; the other saw the bars. It all depends on your attitude, doesn't it? Contentment is an inside job. You will either be a master or a victim of your attitude.

-Wayne Cordeiro

chapter six

THE MANURE
AND THE MUD

"If you're gonna pray for rain, don't complain about a little mud!"

It made a great sermon when my pastor preached it. Years later, though, while bending to the breaking point under the pressure of leadership, it didn't sound quite as clever or cute. I don't remember when the rain started, but I was up to my knees in mud. In fact, I felt like I was caught in a torrential mudslide and I wanted out.

I don't know that I was experiencing anything that any other right-hand man hasn't experienced, but it was sure overwhelming to me. I felt like I was spinning my wheels. I was seeing very little fruit in my leadership. I was frustrated with my senior leaders. I was beginning to doubt that the Lord had really called me to my assignment. I wanted to cry. I wanted to quit.

I don't think I was facing any unusual challenges or crises (although I've certainly faced my share). I think it was just that the realities of leading in the number two position had pushed me to the breaking point. Oh yeah, there was probably one other dynamic at play. I'm sure there was a little demonic oppression thrown into the mix.

The devil hates you, you know. His greatest delight is to see leaders fall. If he can't take you out through an overt attack, he will assail your mind with seeds of discouragement and despair. When I got alone and poured my soul out to the Lord, it didn't sound like me—it sounded like the devil:

"That's it! I'm done! I've spun my wheels long enough and I've stood as long as I can stand. If I've failed, that's fine, but I just can't take it anymore. This is not what I signed up for. I'm willing to work hard and do my best but I'm miserable. I quit."

Please hear my heart! I'm not saying it is demonic to be honest about our emotions and struggles. It's actually very healthy to do so. A cursory read of the psalms of David reveals a leader who was very comfortable expressing his deepest anguish to the Lord. What the enemy loves to do is fuel those feelings of hopelessness until we are convinced that the only option is to run. That's where it becomes demonic.

It's crucial that we recognize our enemy's scheme against our success so we can effectively counterpunch. One of his greatest schemes in attacking right-hand men is to work through the weaknesses of their senior leaders.

Don't worry here! I'm not going to be critical of senior leaders in this chapter and I'm not going to try to rile up your frustrations. But I am going to be honest. It can be a great challenge to serve as a right-hand man, and it wouldn't be fair to leave the challenge unaddressed.

Your leaders are awesome! You wouldn't be serving them if they weren't. You wouldn't allow your reputation to be tied to theirs if you didn't believe in them as strongly as you do. I'm sure you admire them deeply and respect the special gifting and anointing that the Lord has placed on their lives. They're called of God. They're incredibly strong in certain areas.

They're also very human. And they have blind spots.

I doubt very much that there is a perfect leader anywhere in the world. I'm sure that the most wonderful, loving, and efficient leaders you can imagine have some rough spots. There's probably a side to them that has a way of galling their right-hand man.

I love my leaders. I wouldn't be laying my life down for them if I didn't. I'm proud to stand along their side. But they have some blind spots. And the hard part about it is that they don't even realize it. They have some rough edges. They probably have no idea that I can get my feelings hurt by some of their comments (or lack of comments). They probably don't realize that certain interactions we have bring discouragement down upon me. They would never do it intentionally. I know that.

One thing that helps me keep my hurt and frustration in perspective is the fact that I, too, have blind spots. Mine might be worse than theirs. Who knows? That's the thing about blind spots—you can't see them and most people are afraid to point them out to you (at least in a constructive manner).

Let's talk about one of the most common feelings that can descend upon the associate's soul and analyze some keys in processing it.

Keep in mind, as we discuss this, that the enemy wants to instigate and fuel negative emotions in your heart. We can't take all of our frustrations at face value. There *is* a devil who wants nothing more than to derail leaders. If he can get to you, he can hurt your leader and your organization. You're one of his biggest targets. He is constantly amplifying hurt and irritation in you. He's trying to push your buttons. Knowing this, then, and with a heart of grace and understanding, let's look at one of the most common afflictions of the right-hand man's soul.

The second in command can often feel unappreciated. They work very hard. They are often a major part of the backbone of the organization. If the backbone does a good job in the body, it is unnoticed. However, when it's out of place, it gets noticed immediately. This is often the case with the second in command.

They're sort of like sound technicians in a corporate gathering. When everything runs smoothly they are unnoticed, but if a monitor squeals or a microphone won't work, the whole assembly turns to stare at them. The praise goes to the up-front leader while the assistant is often overlooked. The platform personality is the one who is recognized and lauded with thanks and appreciation while the assistant is often the one who has handled the nuts and bolts of the event.

I realize that Paul exhorted the church at Colosse to do their work "not with eye-service as man pleasers but with singleness of heart, fearing God."(Colossians 3:22) I know that I should live my life for an audience of *One* and that *His* "well done" is the only one that I should desire. The problem is that I don't. I want to, but I'm not there yet. I still want to be thanked. I want my leaders to recognize the job that I do, and I want to be appreciated.

I sacrifice a lot. My family has determined that we will live our lives for the sake of God's calling and for no other reason. That requires some selflessness. It mandates some unconditional love. It gets hard sometimes.

I realize that a mature Christian leader should be happy to serve in obscurity and, hopefully, someday I'll get to that selfless state of mind. Until I do, however, I need some help navigating the minefield of hurt and frustration that occurs when I feel that I'm not appreciated or recognized for the work I do. In case you wrestle with that too at times, I've offered a few thoughts to help us with it.

First, recognize that the standard that I just shared about selfless servanthood is the standard for your leadership. Jesus told us that when we do our spiritual duty we should simply say that we were merely doing our obligation as servants.

We *are* servants. We *do* work and serve for Him and Him alone. When I serve my senior leader, I'm really serving Jesus. If my eyes are on man, I'll see humanity and flesh, but if my eyes are on Jesus, I'll see Jesus in my leader. Serving him, then, will become an honor not a chore.

I love First Corinthians 7:22 where Paul says, "*He who was called in the Lord while a slave, is the Lord's freedman.*" True freedom is found in servanthood.

Second, it helps me to remember that my senior leader carries a weight that I know nothing of. As much as I genuinely own and carry the vision, I'm not in his position. The buck doesn't stop with me—it stops with him, and that is a heavy responsibility.

I may do the bulk of the behind-the-scenes work, but people visit our church because of the incredible gifting of our senior pastor. The founder of a company is the reason that the company exists—even if the vice president oversees all of its daily operations. This consistent reminder of the value of your leader to your organization keeps grace and perspective fresh in your mind.

Third, I have to remind myself that my boss can't read my mind. I know this might sound like marriage counseling 101, but it's true. Sometimes I feel unappreciated but I have never shared that I need to feel appreciated. To take it a step further, I've never shared how I most deeply feel and receive appreciation. Have you?

Do you receive affirmation and encouragement verbally or do you prefer to receive a card or a gift? Are you a quality time person or are you content with a slap on the back? Does your boss know the answer to these questions? Have you ever told him?

It dawned on me one day when I was feeling particularly overlooked and unappreciated that my senior leader had no clue that I needed to hear a word of gratitude from him. His assumption was that I knew how he felt about me and my service. He didn't realize how much weight his words carried in affirming my soul. I had never told him.

Here's how I broached the subject. I simply said, "I need to share my heart with you regarding something I've been feeling. I haven't received any feedback from you about…and it's making me wonder if you're pleased with my work. I feel secure in our relationship and I don't need constant affirmation; however, my primary means of receiving encouragement is through words. It means a lot more to me than you probably realize when you simply say, 'You did well on that task' or 'Good job with that meeting.'" It went great! He didn't feel a pressure to pander to me but he became more sensitive to minister to me through verbal encouragement.

In addition to informing them of our personal love language, we should be sure to learn *theirs* as well. Perhaps they *are* expressing appreciation to you—just not in ways that you relate to.

We should be growing in our selflessness and we should be content to serve simply for the glory of God. While we grow into this, however, the enemy attacks us, and it is far better to tactfully and respectfully broach the subject of our frustrations than to take counsel with our speculations and fears.

Having said this, let me now switch directions. Although it is highly important to provide your leader with insight to the needs of your heart, we must remember that there are some needs that a senior leader will never be able to meet. My leaders are not God. There will always be a Jesus-shaped hole in my heart that only He can complete.

One of my favorite Scripture verses is Colossians 2:10 that says: "*In Him you have been made complete.*" The definition of the word *complete* references a house that is filled with a sweet perfume or a net that is filled with fish. In other words, he said that when we are truly surrounded by Jesus, our lives become filled with purpose and a sweet fragrance. He (Jesus), not a word of affirmation from my leader, completes me.

I'm a firm believer that we, as sons and daughters of God, represent Jesus to those around us. In a very real sense we become His hands and feet on planet Earth; however, every person still needs Him directly. They need to feel the reality of His presence and hear the soft sweetness of His voice.

The Lord wants us to be dependent on *Him*. Consequently, there are probably times when He sees to it that our leaders let us down. Every leader will disappoint a follower from time to time. Woe to that follower if his or her faith rested solely in the leader.

Paul said, "*Follow me as I follow Christ,*" but he never asked his followers to put their ultimate hope in him. He knew that people need Jesus. As leaders we must constantly lead people back to Him.

Certainly, God uses our leaders to speak to us and mentor us. In some ways they become a very real extension of His presence and work in our lives; however, there will be times in the life of every leader where he must find God alone. (The next chapter will address the issue of how to find Him.)

There is another reason that God allows our leaders to be incomplete vessels in ministering to our souls. He is training us. If our leaders were able to meet our every need and perfectly help us in every situation, they might preempt some opportunities for growth in our lives.

I received a birthday card from my uncle when I turned 16. Pardon the crassness, but it said, "I know the grass probably looks greener in someone else's yard…but chances are it has just as much dog manure as your own." Although this may sound terribly rude and critical, please let me use it to illustrate a point. The sentiment of this birthday card is true of your service of your senior leaders.

The thought can frequently arise in our hearts that service in another field might be more fulfilling. Another organization may appear to be strong in the areas that yours is struggling, and the thoughts can emerge: "I bet it's much easier to lead over there." Can you take a guess as to whose voice that might be? It's not yours. It's certainly not your Father's.

Here are a couple of keys to overcoming the voice of the adversary and navigating through the inevitable challenges that you will have with your leader:

1. Remember that you, too, have blind spots.

2. Remember that your leader carries a pressure that the right-hand man doesn't experience (no matter how fully he owns the vision).

3. Remember that God is at work in you.

4. Remember that one of the tools that He uses for this work is your senior leader.

5. Remember that you must articulate your needs to your senior leader—he cannot read your mind.

6. Remember that no matter how wonderful your leader may or may not be, there are areas of your heart that can only be touched and encouraged by Jesus Himself.

7. Remember that you are complete only in Christ.

8. Remember that if you respond to His work at this level it will qualify you for promotion.

9. Lastly, remember that the Lord assigned you to your current position because He believed that you were perfect for it.

He's answered your prayer! He's sent you where you're needed most! Your company needs you! Your ministry needs you! His scepter is outstretched to you.

Your net worth to the world is usually determined by what remains after your bad habits are subtracted from your good ones.

-Benjamin Franklin

It seems, in fact, as though the second half of a man's life is made up of nothing but the habits he has accumulated during the first half.

-Fyodor Mikhaylovich Dostoyevsky

Spiritual leadership requires Spirit-filled people. Other qualities are important; to be Spirit-filled is indispensable.

-J. Oswald Sanders

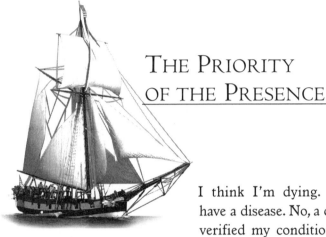

THE PRIORITY
OF THE PRESENCE

I think I'm dying. I definitely have a disease. No, a doctor hasn't verified my condition, but I can feel it overtaking me. It's crippling all of my efforts to move. It's haunting me.

I think about it all of the time. I know I need to make some changes to my lifestyle because I'm succumbing to its paralysis.

It's affecting my performance (I was a much better leader before it gained a foothold in me). It's affecting my marriage (I've been floundering as a husband since it started its rampage through my soul).

It hurts. It slows me down. It makes me easily agitated. It sucks the life out of me. Since I became infected, I've been struggling with it every day. In fact, I'm wrestling with it right now.

It's ugly. I'm ashamed to talk about it. I interacted with people much more easily before I was diagnosed. Now, I'm a little insecure. My confidence has been rapidly disappearing and I'm beginning to doubt myself. I can't remember exactly when it began but I can certainly feel the effects of it.

Did I mention that this isn't my first bout with it? Actually, I've struggled off-and-on with this for a long time. I've had several close calls, but it's gone into remission each time. I thought that I finally had it beat.

I had done so well for so long. There hadn't been any recurrences for many months and I was just beginning to enjoy my new life. I felt strong. I was happy. Now look at me. I'm ruined.

I should warn you: It's contagious. Especially for leaders.

My discouragement level is at an all-time low. My vision has blurred so much that I've almost forgotten my name and I so badly wish I could quit. The worst thing about my condition, though, is that it's self-inflicted.

I did it to myself.

I can't blame anyone but me. I didn't catch this from my kids. It wasn't passed on to me by someone at work. No, I'm the only guilty party. It's completely my fault.

I stopped praying.

And as if that's not enough, I added to my own hurt when I became too busy. At least I think that's how it happened. It may have been reversed. I might have become too busy to pray. Either way, it's gotten me.

Prayerlessness is killing me.

It started with my perspective. It always begins there. I began seeing things from my natural, worldly perspective. I lost focus on God's bird's-eye view of things. Instead of perceiving His purposes and handiwork behind circumstances, I began to view them as isolated, independent events. Consequently, I became frustrated. I didn't have the grace for people and situations that I usually have. I was more impatient and impulsive. I lost my sense of purpose. My confidence soon followed.

As my courage ebbed, I felt an increasing sense of insecurity and intimidation. I became reluctant to pioneer new ventures. I waffled in my self-confidence. I started to sit back and let others lead. My judgment became skewed.

Although I couldn't see it at the time, it's very clear to me today that I began to filter situations through a grid of fear. My decisions became fear based. I began to think defensively and fantasize about worst-case scenarios. I feared that failure was imminent.

As criticisms and complaints reached my ears (they always seem to find their way to the leader's ears), I began to trust them more than I trusted the Word of God. With this faulty judgment I saw a red alert when things were probably (at worst) only a yellow level. This skewed perspective inevitably led to ineffectiveness.

Leaders can't lead when their perspective is tainted by fear and frustration. They can't lead when relying on their own ability. The ultimate foretelling of doom for a Christian leader is when they begin to lead primarily out of their personalities instead of the anointing.

That was me. Prayerlessness had so gripped my life that I began to offer people insights from my own soul instead of life-giving words from the Holy Spirit. For a pastor, that's a deadly trap.

When my disease had fully blossomed and had a choke-hold on my soul, I was ready to quit. I was ready to die. I doubted God. I doubted my calling. If this was the abundant life that Jesus promised, then someone else was welcome to it. I must have been mistaken when I thought He had called me to lead. After all, leaders take most of the arrows, and I was feeling like a big red target for practicing archers. I just wanted out.

Ever been there? Have you ever lost perspective and grace and courage and only after days or weeks or months of spiraling, realized that it all started when the demands of leadership drove you out of your prayer closet? Have you ever been too busy to pray? Have you ever suffered the consequences? Has the Holy Spirit ever diagnosed the state of your soul as being overrun by the disease of prayerlessness? Thankfully, there is a cure.

It's really quite simple.

Pray. Repent. Return. He hasn't left you. He's still waiting.

In Song of Solomon 1:4 the bride says, in essence, *"Draw me; we will run together."* It's impossible to run the race and fight the fight and pursue the vision in our own ability. He must draw us.

I've always been very faithful in my daily devotions. I love the Bible and I love the presence of the Lord. Consequently, it has been fairly easy for me to develop a pretty consistent plan for Bible study and prayer. My problem has been that it's ended there.

On a whim (probably a Spirit-led one), I did a study one day of all of the instances that Jesus withdrew from the crowds to pray. I was trying to gain more balance in my personal schedule and carve out more time to pray, and I thought it might help me to study the prayer habits of Jesus. I wondered if He demonstrated a pattern that I could follow. I was facing several large decisions and I felt that I needed an extra dose of His presence. Here's what I found.

Constant communion with the Father was the benchmark of Jesus' spirituality. He never did or said anything apart from what He saw or heard His Father doing. He truly lived Paul's exhortation to pray without ceasing; however, He didn't stop there. Although He always communed with the Father, He consistently withdrew for strategic, intensified prayer. He did this when facing eight specific situations:

1. When in need of direction in His ministry.

2. When experiencing increased growth/expansion in His ministry.

3. When selecting/placing leaders in the ministry.

4. When commissioning His leaders for specific ministry tasks.

5. When weary and grieving.

6. When tempted to lose heart.

7. When His followers were battling a storm.

8. Prior to facing the cross.

I was shocked and mortified when I completed this summary because I, personally, was facing six out of these eight scenarios and yet I was taking *no* additional time for prayer. I was simply living out of the strength of my daily devotions.

That's bad enough.

It's even worse when leaders live out of the strength of their personality and their leadership ability. I heard a question asked once in a sermon that has lodged in my mind: "If the Holy Spirit backed completely out of your ministry, would things carry on as usual?"

Is the presence of God your priority? Is the glory of God central to your business? Remember that God was very intentional when He instructed Moses to geographically arrange the 12 tribes of Israel while they were traveling in the desert. He had them structured in a balanced arrangement where three tribes lined up in each direction. Three tribes lined up to the north, three tribes lined up to south, east, and west. The prominent feature of this arrangement was that the Tabernacle, that housed the glory of God, was placed in the center of the 12 tribes. At the center of the daily life of Israel was the presence and glory of God.

Don't you think a church would grow and flourish with God at its center? Isn't it ludicrous to think that a church could grow without Him? Yet it happens all of the time. Programs replace the presence. Vision replaces His voice.

Do you remember Obed-Edom? He was the fellow who housed the Ark of the Covenant for three months while King David contemplated how to bring it back to Jerusalem. Do you remember what the Bible says of Obed-Edom? It says, "*The Lord blessed Obed-Edom and all of his household*" (2 Sam. 6:11). The quickest way to the blessing is to house the presence of God. Does your ministry do that? Is your company a holding tank for the glory or is it merely a means to a prosperous end? Remember, prosperity lies *with Him*.

It's very easy for associate level leaders to fall prey to the tyranny of the urgent. After all, their job is to keep the details of the machine running. Their eye needs to stay on all of the components of the corporation to ensure its efficiency and success. Let me shatter a myth: It is not only the senior leader (of a church or a business or a school or a medical practice) that needs to go to the mountaintop to hear the word of the Lord for the organization. The right-hand man must go too.

Joshua did.

I remember the story. I know that he didn't get to experience everything that Moses did on Mount Sinai-Joshua had to sit outside the cloud for 30 days while Moses was inside with the Lord. There is a special place for the senior leader to hear from the Lord and to receive divine direction for the company. However, it's not God's primary choice to have him do it entirely alone. Moses took Joshua. Jesus took three disciples.

If life and business as usual have led you into a fast-paced, detail-oriented existence, I encourage you to get alone with the Lord. In the eight instances when Jesus took extra time to pray, it was often said that He "withdrew" to pray. Withdraw from busyness. Withdraw from day timers and cell phones so you can seek the face of your Father.

He is the one who holds the keys of prosperity for your business. He will provide for the growth of your church. He wants to mentor you. The only thing stopping Him from having His way in your life is *you*.

Satan can't keep my Father from mentoring me. Satan can't keep my Father from giving me the keys of the Kingdom of Heaven. He can't keep me from experiencing my Father's love and training and blessing.

But I can.

I can get too busy. I can trust my personality more than His presence. I can lead from charisma instead of the secret place.

I can be a Martha.

Do you remember her? She was the lady who busily prepared the meal for Jesus while her sister, Mary, sat and spoke with Jesus.

She would make a perfect vice president. She would make a perfect executive pastor. She would be the perfect right-hand man. She's a self-starter. She's motivated. Give her a task and it's done. She needs very little oversight. She's able to multitask. Everything she does carries the mark of excellence. She loves God. She can be trusted. She only has one flaw.

She's too busy.

Would you mind spying on her with me? She's working right now. She has a full house. In fact, Jesus is there. Let's walk through her familiar Bible story and weave imagination with literal interpretations of the words. The Scripture references read as follows:

> *Now as they were traveling along, He entered a certain village; and a woman named Martha welcomed Him into her home. And she had a sister called Mary, who moreover was listening to the Lord's word, seated at His feet. But Martha was distracted with all her preparations; and she came up to Him and said, "Lord, do you not care that my sister has left me to do all the serving alone? Then tell her to help me." But the Lord answered her and said to her, "Martha, Martha, you are worried and bothered about so many things; but only a few things are necessary, really only one, for Mary has chosen the good part, which shall not be taken away from her"* (Luke 10:38-42).

Incidentally, this particular story occurs immediately after Jesus finished sharing His famous story about the Good Samaritan. Once He left Martha's house, He began to teach His followers about spiritual warfare and intercession (see Luke 10:30-11:13). It's interesting that His interaction with Martha and Mary is a bridge that spans between the two. Perhaps there is a word to us through these Scriptures, that if we don't learn the lessons from Martha and Mary, both our Good Samaritan ministry and our intercessory prayer ministry might be short-lived.

Anyway, Jesus had been traveling. He and the boys were tired, hot, and hungry when they made their way to Martha's home. Our text told us that she *welcomed* them into her home. The word *welcome* means to receive kindly with hospitality.

Jesus entered Martha's house and immediately experienced the refreshing, cathartic gift of hospitality. Don't you love people with the gift of hospitality? I do. I love to be pampered and appreciated and cared for when I visit in their homes. Hospitality people have the ability to make you feel like the most important person on the planet. It's a gift. My wife has the gift of hospitality. It's a wonderful gift that is desperately needed in our society and culture.

Martha was wonderful! And she had a sister.

Thank God, she had a sister! Her sister saved her. You see, she was suffering from our disease. Imagine what our story would sound like without Mary: "*As they were traveling, they entered a certain village and a certain woman named Martha welcomed them in, fed them, refreshed them, and sent them on their way.*"

Sadly, that's the way it is with many churches and businesses.

Well, thank God for Mary. In the middle of this story there is a little tangent inserted. *Martha needed Mary!* This story is all about courting the presence of the Lord. Our leadership success hinges on our ability to court and sustain the presence of the Lord in our organizations. However, you and I can't do it alone. We need a Mary.

For us to walk in the fullness of our relationships with God, we need a brother or a sister. We need their encouragement and love. We need their iron-sharpening-iron effect in our lives. We need them to help us find the feet of Jesus.

Of course we need to have our own personal, private walk with God and without it, no amount of fellowship with people can sustain us, and yet we all know that the gospel is a relational story. We need each other. You need Mary.

And you need *to be* a Mary. You are destined to help someone else find their place at Jesus' feet where they can see into His eyes and hear every inflection of His voice.

Apparently, Jesus wanted to talk. While Martha cooked and prepared, Mary sat at Jesus' feet listening to His word. Although He was hungry and tired, what He really wanted to do was share a word with someone.

He has some things He wants to tell *you*. He has some thoughts for your ministry. I know you're a high-ranking leader in your company, but He's still the Head of all things and He has a few observations to pass along to you.

Mary sat at His feet and heard His word.

Martha cooked and cleaned. She probably needed to. After all, her home would house the Master. It probably smelled wonderful when He opened the door. Peter and the boys probably started salivating when their nostrils sampled the fragrance of her hospitality. However, Jesus wanted to talk, and from her place in the kitchen, Martha could only catch muffled tidbits of His words.

She tried to have a good attitude but she was getting very annoyed. Mary hadn't even lifted a finger. She hadn't offered to serve any of the guests. She just plopped down at His feet and ignored everyone else. After a while, Martha couldn't take it anymore.

"Lord, don't You care that my sister has left me to do all of the work alone…then tell her to help me." The fact that she uses the word *then*, implies that Jesus responded to her question. It seems that He said that, yes, He did care that Martha was left to do the work alone. What Martha didn't realize was that He *did* tell Mary to help her. Mary was helping her far more than she realized.

I love how Jesus addressed Martha. He said, "Martha, Martha…." I love that He said her name twice. It implies such tenderness and kind regard. He said, "Martha, I do care about you. In fact, I'm worried about you. You're distracted and encumbered with all of your pressing needs. You're dragging a heavy burden behind you. I'm surprised you can move so quickly about your house with this great weight attached to your heart and your mind. Oh, I know that what you're carrying is a desire to *serve*. I know that you want to minister compassionate love to the needy, but your great love for people has made you vulnerable. You're dragging around the hurts of humanity. You're dragging around the needs of those who you care for.

"Martha, you're troubled. There is a wailing clamor in your mind. Your great concern and anxiety is causing you to become disunited in your heart. I know this has all happened innocently (that's usually how it begins), but you've entirely missed the point of My visit. Martha, I came to see *you*.

"Since you've gotten so busy, your discernment is slipping (that's a sign of chronic busyness). I'm not hungry at all. I didn't come to your home for your great cooking. I didn't come here to take advantage of your hospitality. I missed you. I wanted to be with you. I have a word to share. I appreciate your heart to serve Me but I didn't ask you for a meal. Martha, there's really only one thing that is necessary."

It's still true today. Only one thing is necessary. By the way, this isn't just a word for pastors. It's a word for *leaders*.

Only one thing is necessary for anyone who cares about people.

Only one thing is necessary for anyone who wants to see the Kingdom of God expand in the earth.

Only one thing is necessary for anyone who loves the Body of Christ.

Yes, I know that there are wounded people lying in the ditch on the road to Jericho. I know that there are deadlines to reach and contracts to sign. I know the needs of your church clamor for your attention. I know there is a lot to *do*, but the word is still the same: Only one thing is needful.

Mary wasn't being lazy when she listened to His word. The word *listened* means to hear with understanding so you can obey and *do* effectively. Listening is the precursor for effective action.

Jesus says to us, "Don't spin your wheels in warfare. Don't let the needs around you strangle you. Get My strategy! Sit a while and let Me download the battle plan. Sit at My feet."

Do you remember that the Scripture tells us that the world is His footstool? If He says to sit at His feet, He's really inviting us into His dominion and victory. He's in control of all things. He says, "Sit with Me in victory. Let Me give you My strategy and then go forth in triumph with all of the resources of Heaven at your disposal." By the way, Jesus told Martha that when she was thus postured, nothing could take her place away.

I think my favorite part of the story is verse 43. Oh, I know that your Bible doesn't have that particular verse in it. I made it up. I still think it happened though. Here's what verse 43 would have said:

> *So the salad wilted and the bread burned and Martha wept and wept as Jesus removed the weight of the world from her shoulders.*

He wants to do this for you.

He holds the key to your ministry. He knows how to build Fortune 500 companies.

He has a place for us, but if we're too busy, we're *too busy.*

Satan can't stop a woman like Martha, so he gets her to do more. He probably can't quench your leadership drive, so he'll get behind you and push you. It's not good leadership to be driven by the devil. It's time to withdraw.

Leader, He's waiting for you.

Leadership is a potent combination of strategy and character.
But if you must be without one, be without the strategy.

-General H. Norman Schwarzkopf

The same ambition can destroy or save,
and makes a patriot as it makes a knave.

-Alexander Pope

Our policy is simple: We are not going to betray our friends,
reward the enemies of freedom, or permit fear and retreat to
become American policies…none of the wars in my lifetime
came about because we were too strong.

-Ronald Reagan

FOCUS ON THE FAMILY

Don't forget your family! For the Christian leader, the measurement of success is found within the walls of their own home. I heard someone say that the true definition of success is when those who know you the best, respect you the most. For the Christian, this couldn't be truer. Successful leadership means nothing without the health and support of your family.

I don't think any book on leadership would be complete without a strong admonition to prioritize the priorities. My wife is more important to me than my church. I hope and intend to be active in ministry for my lifetime, but I want to make sure I'm doing it with her. Leadership is a consuming calling and, if unguarded, it can absorb all of the margins in our life.

My daughters are six and three years old. They love to have tea parties with chocolate milk. We toast every member of the family and laugh until we cry. My tea party appointments are more important than my board meetings. A church elder can wait. Amber and Madelyn cannot. It requires great balance and understanding to address this particular aspect of leadership because a true leader is a servant and when God places a call of leadership on an individual's life, their family gets drafted for the assignment too.

As a pastor, I *do* need to be available for the crises of my people. There are certain functions and events that I just can't miss. As pastors or business leaders or medical doctors (or any other high-level leader), you are also inundated with needs that genuinely do need to be met; however, it's very easy for leaders to allow the nonessential needs and demands of the company to encroach upon their priorities.

My priorities all have blue eyes. They're all girls. They all love to laugh. They love me but they aren't all that interested in how my latest strategy session went. They just want me. They want me to be emotionally engaged.

I don't know if other husbands are better at tricking their wives than I am, but I can't seem to fake it when I'm distracted and preoccupied with the details of my job. No matter how fun and conversant I try to be, Jessica knows. She can hear me thinking. She's very understanding, but I don't want her to always *need* to be understanding.

My leadership duties had kicked my rear end one week. I had been in meetings every evening for about ten days straight. I was working hard and getting a lot accomplished, but all I was bringing home was my emotional leftovers. One night in the middle of this stretch of time, I arrived home to find Jessica waiting expectantly for my return. It had been another 12-hour day and I was exhausted. I literally dragged my briefcase behind me into the house and flopped onto the nearest couch with a sigh.

Jessica was completing a phone conversation, but she smiled at me when I came in the door. She has a beautiful smile. When I saw her smile and the sweetness of her expression, a conviction from the Holy Spirit pierced my soul. It was late, but she was waiting up for me. She was hoping to connect. She wasn't even complaining that I had been giving her leftovers.

I knew I had to change.

I jumped to my feet and motioned to her that I would be back momentarily. I raced our car out of our driveway in an attempt to reach Baskin Robbins before they closed. I shouted in the car. I rolled down the windows and let the cold air slap my face until I was fully awake. I repented. I made vows to the Lord that I wouldn't give my highest and best to everyone during the day and then be too spent to bless my family.

Well, I made it to Baskin Robbins and I made it to Blockbuster, and Jessica and I had a wonderful in-house date. Our girls were asleep, and we talked for hours.

I want to grow old with her in ministry. I want her and our girls to know that they are adored. Jess and I are committed to teaching our daughters that it is an honor to serve the Lord and His people; however, we never want them to resent our lifestyle because of our extreme busyness. Yes, we're going to serve and lay our lives down, but we're also going to play the guessing game. We're going to have picnics and we're going to shop. They're going to love ministry. They're going to think that leadership is a pretty good deal.

You see, they're really all I have. If I lose them, I lose my ministry.

It's possible for an unsaved corporate executive to neglect certain areas of family priorities or personal morality and continue to make a financial profit. As Christian leaders, though, we can't lose our families and then carry on as if nothing has happened. Our credibility is dependent on how well we cultivate and cover those closest to us.

In addition to maintaining and growing a strong family complete with traditions and dates and memories, Jessica and I also want to develop some close friendships. We've decided that we don't want to try to live and lead alone. We want to grow old with some like-minded, covenant friends.

I grew up in a small, rural town where community was everything. Our life revolved around church and community events and the deepest of friendships. I seem to recall falling asleep at friends' homes nearly every evening while our parents laughed and talked late into the evening. I want that. I want my girls to experience that depth of friendship and love.

One of the young adult leaders in our church commented that a problem with America today is the size of our front porches. They're shrinking. It used to be (and it was in my childhood) that life occurred with friends and family on the front porch as stories were shared and life was lived in community.

Unfortunately, the incredible demands of leadership make it very difficult to cultivate those levels of relationship. I'm called to lead and impact the world. So are you. If we want these types of relationships, they must be intentionally formed and facilitated, and that takes time—which is a commodity of the highest premium for the leader.

I know that everyone is busy. Our culture today is frantically paced and it is only picking up steam. My cell phone seems intent on disrupting any solitude I try to attain. Often, when I think I've completed my ever-growing to-do list, I'll realize that I've forgotten to return about 20 E-mails. When I finally complete my daily tasks, I'm ready to give all of my remaining time to my family and friends.

In my position as executive pastor in the church, I'm constantly juggling the requests of my senior leader with the needs of the staff members as well as the needs of the congregation. I'm stretched in three different directions.

I want to be a world-class executive pastor who makes my leaders proud. I want them to wonder how they ever functioned before I became a part of the team. I want them to feel served and loved and supported. I want them to feel honored and safe and well-represented to our people.

I also want to be an excellent leader for the leadership team around me. I want my leaders to feel that they have landed on a gold mine in my organization. I want them to thank God every day that He has allowed them to work here. They're wonderful leaders, and I want them to feel appreciated and strengthened.

In addition to serving those above me and those around me, I also serve ministry leaders in the church and individual members of the congregation. I love them! It's the greatest privilege of my life to serve these people and to attempt to strengthen their relationship with Jesus. I hope they discover who God has made them to be and find deep satisfaction in pursuing His plan for their lives. I want them to love serving in our church. They are a great assembly of people!

The only problem is that I could spend nearly all of my time wearing any one of these leadership hats. I could work full time just maintaining the status quo of these three ministry venues. And you well know that leaders hate the status quo. We're called to bring change. We're called to advance. I want to take good care of my senior leaders and my staff and our congregation but I also want to make tangible progress. I want to find innovative new ways to reach the city of Colorado Springs with the gospel. I want to grow in my understanding of church life and how to penetrate today's culture with a relevant message. I want to make sure that no one falls through the cracks in our church. I want everyone to build relationships and find fulfilling outlets for ministry. I want the church to grow. I have a lot to do.

Oh, I realize that I'm probably carrying more than I need to. I might be trying to do too much. But you probably are too. That's the way it is with leaders—especially the second-in-command leaders. The right-hand man wants to make their boss look good and fulfill their desires for the company. They want to complete all of the tasks and vision of the leader. However, they themselves are also high level leaders so they want to ensure that their own desires and standards of excellence are performed.

My point in all of this is not to whine about my schedule. You're every bit as busy as I am. I'm sharing all of this in order to loudly yell that *things must change.* You will be a better, more loving, more excellent leader if you lead from a place of rest. If you take time to refresh your family and your own soul, you will add far more value to your organization.

Jessica and I have learned a powerful principle that has helped us retain the priority of preserving family time. It's actually a frightening principle, and we've learned it the hard way. Simply stated it is this: *Excessive busyness opens the door for demonic attack.* Let me draw you into one of the worst nights of my leadership experience and then I'll discuss this dynamic.

I had come home late. Jess and the girls were already asleep. It had been a good day. I felt like I had helped some people. I was encouraged about the state of the various ministries in the church. I was happy. Plus, there was a letter waiting for me on the counter when I got home. Jessica is wonderful about writing notes and cards, so I was excited as I anticipated what I thought would be a sweet love letter. I was wrong.

It's not that the letter wasn't sweet (Jessica is one of the purest, mercy-motivated people I know), but it was laced with steel. It wasn't an ultimatum letter, but it certainly got my attention. Our life had to change. The pressures of life and ministry had begun to take their toll and our family was growing weary. The joy had been steadily slipping out of our lives. Our love was as deep as ever, but we were losing the thrill of serving God and His people. We were trapped on a treadmill of endless meetings with no real relationships to show for it. We were faithfully giving our lives but we weren't really living our lives.

I'm not a workaholic by nature. Although a lot of great leaders struggle in this area, it's not my nature to lose myself in my career. I'm a family man. My favorite thing is to jump on the trampoline with my girls. I love to be home. However, as I've stated, the demands of leadership can pull anyone into the tyranny of the urgent. By the way, that's exactly what it is: tyranny. I had become enslaved.

What I realized from studying Jessica's letter (and from subsequent prayer and conversations) was that we were under a full-scale demonic attack. We learned in that season that if we allowed our life to lose the rhythm of grace we would become vulnerable to our enemy.

Jesus promised us an abundant life. In John 10:10, He said that He had come that we might have life and *"life more abundantly."* I love how Eugene Peterson paraphrased Matthew 11:29. He said that Jesus is calling us to *"learn the unforced rhythms of grace"* (TM). Somehow we had lost the rhythm.

Satan will attack us with any means possible. He's just as happy with burnout as he is adultery. If he can't get you to renounce God, he'll just get you to burn out in the service of God. If God is blessing your business and satan can't hurt you economically, he'll try to keep you so busy that you can't enjoy the blessings.

He knows that blessings can act like curses if not handled properly. A growing church is a wonderful blessing, but it is also a greatly increased workload. A successful business is every businessperson's dream; however, when the dream comes true there are many more customers with needs, expectations, concerns, and potential problems.

The writer of the Proverbs said, *"The blessing of the Lord...makes rich and He adds no sorrow to it."* The Lord intends for His blessings to enrich our lives. Satan tries to get them to enslave our lives with added sorrow.

When I left my business and was ordained and installed in my current ministry position, one of my mentors said to me, "Call me when your dreams come true. That's when you'll really need me." I didn't understand what he meant until I read Jessica's letter. My dream had come true—and my family was miserable.

That letter from Jessica kept me up all night. But it changed my life. It really was a love letter. Sometimes love hurts before it can heal.

Not only did I realize that busyness was taking a toll on us in practical and emotional ways, but I also began to see how we were being spiritually affected. The biblical pattern that the Lord used to shed light into our situation was the study of Elijah's encounter with Queen Jezebel.

The prophet Elijah had done great things for the Lord. He had killed the Lord's enemies and performed signs and wonders by the hand of God. He was a success. He called down the fire of God and he outran the king's chariot. However, he also reached a point of emotional and physical exhaustion that precipitated his vulnerability to Jezebel's attack.

In a mere moment in time, Elijah switched from having unflinching confidence in God to being discouraged to the point of death. When he listened to the threats delivered by Jezebel's messenger, a spiritual force seeped into the exhausted places of his heart and he eventually wanted to die. In fact, if you take a close look at the passage you see that it took divine food, days of rest, and a visitation from God to revive him.

Jessica and I have found that when we lose the rhythm of grace we become more vulnerable to the Jezebel-like effects of spiritual warfare. Do you remember some of those effects? Here are a few: discouragement, loneliness, feelings of isolation, the sense that your labor is in vain, despair, the sense that you have been forgotten by God, fear, the desire to quit and, if unchecked, the desire to die. That's pretty heavy isn't it? Does it seem dramatic to place this much emphasis and power on a simple principle like time management? I don't think so. You probably don't either. I would wager that you have experienced most of these effects of Jezebel at some time in your career.

It's a simple fact that when people are worn out they are more vulnerable. This vulnerability is not just physical or emotional, however. It's spiritual. When a couple takes regular time for conversation, dates, and prayer, they create a shield that the enemy cannot penetrate. It's when the pace of life eliminates the time for that heart connection that fears and mental doubts can ensue.

Communication dispels fear. If a couple is too busy to regularly communicate, they become vulnerable to suggestions and impressions from the enemy.

One of the purposes of the Sabbath rest is to restore the rhythm of life so the doors of access are closed to the enemy of our souls. Having time to play with your children shuts a door to fear. Of course Dad loves me! He plays with me every day when he gets home. Of course Mom thinks I'm great! She tells me all the time.

You and I *do* have time to fulfill the will of God for our lives. Although He asks us take up our cross and follow Him, He doesn't ask us to sacrifice our families on the altar of busy service. He has called you to a specific task in His Kingdom. It might be in the marketplace or it might be in the church. It might be in a medical clinic or it might be in Hollywood. Regardless of what He's called you to and the demands that the calling entails, *there is still time to live.*

Now, I'm not trying to be overly simplistic. I know it's hard to take control of our schedules. It's a never-ending challenge for a leader to balance the demands of the organization and the needs of the family. However, it *can* be done.

I was praying about this issue recently and I felt inspired to read the account of the Creation of the world. I always love to read the Genesis account about how the Lord spoke all things into existence. There are fascinating studies available to us in the first few chapters of the Bible. On this particular day I was checking in with the Lord to see how I was doing in my different callings.

My first calling is as a Christian. After that I'm called as a husband and a father. Finally, I'm a pastor. I felt like I had been doing better at fulfilling my callings and maintaining the rhythm but I wanted to see if the Lord would show me anything I might have been missing. What He showed me was wonderful.

As I read the first chapter in Genesis, I was struck by the fifth verse where God called the evening and the morning the first day. I realized that in one of the first glimpses we have of God in the Bible we see Him taking authority over time. We see Him telling time what it will be called and where it will go and what it will do when it gets there. "Evening and morning," He said, "you're one day."

I realized then that I could do the same thing. My master is Jesus. I shouldn't be enslaved to anything but Him. I don't have to be the servant of time. I can tell it where to go. I can walk in dominion and use it as my slave.

So can you.

How do you do it? It's not easy. It's hard for leaders to manage the various roles of their lives and take time to be refreshed when so much is expected of them. It's a great challenge to withdraw for rest and rejuvenation when the bottom line is directly linked to their efforts.

It's hard for all leaders, but I think it's especially difficult for business owners.

Business owners often feel enslaved to the demands of their business. If they take a vacation, they feel a need to check in. They're always on call. They're always available for the needs of their employees and customers.

Let me share some of the practical things Jessica and I have done to take dominion over our time.

First, we identified the things that are essential for the health of our marriage and family. For us, that entails daily couch time (where we cuddle up with coffee and talk), weekly dates, time invested in friendships, and large doses of play time and laughter with our young daughters.

In addition to all of this, Jessica needs a break from the girls. Stay-at-home moms (and single parents) are probably the hardest workers of any group. Whenever I take the girls for an entire day, I am humbled and renewed in my admiration for Jessica and how hard she works. I often try to magnify this many times over in my mind and imagine the sacrificial living that is done by single parents. They're amazing!

Jessica needs a break. She needs to laugh and, sadly for me, she likes to shop. She needs to socialize with friends. I, however, need solitude. I need time to think and process and be alone. To fulfill my ministry calling, I need to spend a lot of time with the Lord in prayer and study.

As we analyzed the state of our life, we prioritized all of the above. We asked the simple question: "What are the activities that we *must* have in any given week that enable us to stay refreshed, emotionally strong, and inspired to do the work the Lord has assigned to us?" Then we built our life around those activities.

It's still a fight. It seems that if we slack off for even one week we're back on the slippery slope of busyness and discouragement. If I lose dominion over time, I can feel those missiles of the enemy launched at my soul, but at least I'm learning how to recognize them now. I'm learning to keep the door closed. Thankfully, I'm learning how to get off the treadmill.

94

I don't have time for everything, but I do have time to obey the Lord. I have time to please my heavenly Father. I might have to skip the season premiere of the latest reality television show, but *I can be* a faithful Christian, husband, father, pastor, and friend. I can be faithful to my calling.

So can you!

It's crucial that we do—especially in light of the next topic.

The nation will find it very hard to look up to the leaders who are keeping their ears to the ground.

-Sir Winston Leonard Spencer Churchill

A true leader has the confidence to stand alone, the courage to make tough decisions, and the compassion to listen to the needs of others. He does not set out to be a leader, but becomes one by the equality of his actions and the integrity of his intent.

-Douglas McCarther

Those who have attained things worth having in this world have worked while others idled, have persevered when others gave up in despair, have practiced early in life the valuable habits of self-denial, industry, and singleness of purpose. As a result, they enjoy in later life the success so often erroneously attributed to good luck.

-Grenville Kleiser

Successful men do daily what unsuccessful men do occasionally.

-Pastor Brent Sparks

I OWN THIS THING

Effective associate leaders do not work for pay. They own the organization. Oh, they might be salaried employees with a set work schedule and clearly defined job duties; however, they are far more than employees. They are owners. The company is just as much theirs as it is the literal owner's.

It has to be this way. Too much rests on the associate's shoulders for them to be a mere hireling. The weight of responsibility is far too great to be carried by a hired hand. Only an owner, who truly lives for the success of the organization, can adequately implement the dream. Owning a company or leading a ministry requires a lot of sacrifice from the leader. Great works are not built on banker's hours.

In saying this, I'm not advocating the plague of workaholism. I'm speaking to the heart attitude. As I've previously discussed, I prize my family time above all else. I'm determined to be there while my daughters grow up. Theirs will not be the testimony of an absent father. Having said this, though, I am fully aware that I'll never accomplish anything great for God if I approach my work as a mere employee.

Let me clarify what I mean. Employees log time in exchange for a paycheck. Owners work for an ideal. Hirelings do what must be done to get paid. Visionary leaders work for the furtherance of a dream. I'm grateful when payday rolls around but I didn't respond to the call of God so I could be the employee of a church. I want to change the world.

I want to give my life for something that outlasts me. I want to change the spiritual climate of my generation. I want to leave some fruit that remains. I've experienced some tragedy and I've learned that it has a way of crystallizing purpose.

My wife and I had a beautiful daughter who died when she was three years old. The aftermath of that world-altering experience clarified some things for me. I want to make it to Heaven so I can see her again. I want to love my wife every day of my life. I don't want to waste a single day with my two other daughters. Life is hard. In fact, it's far too hard to just exist in it.

If I'm going to pay a price and lay my life down, I want it to be for a great cause that does some good in the world. Life is too hard to just work for weekends and holidays. Jessica and I love Hawaii, but I've sat on the beaches of Maui and wept in the throes of hard grief. Hawaii is not enough. Retirement is not enough. I want to give a black eye to the evil in the world. I want my life to count.

I heard a haunting phrase escape the lips of a desperate man the other day. His wife had left him and he hadn't seen her in two months. Shocked and reeling, he had begun writing love letters to share his heart with her. The phrase that gripped my soul with the fear of the Lord was when he said to me, "I wish I had started writing these letters to her 18 years ago."

I don't want to approach the twilight years of my life and say, "If only I had lived for a higher purpose. I wish I had pursued what really matters. I should have been writing letters all along."

Owners embrace a present price to secure a future blessing.

Do you own your ministry? Do you own your company? I know you serve your senior leader, but I hope you own the vision every bit as much as he does. You can't be an effective right-hand man unless you do.

When we live this way, there is a weight of responsibility that onlookers do not understand.

Some employees may work longer hours than I do, but I take the vision home. Of course there are perks that come to leaders, but they also live under intense pressure.

One of the most stinging comments to me is when people ask, "What exactly do pastors do all day?" I can assure you we don't just pray and play golf. We're struggling to keep up. We're fighting a multifaceted battle. We are fighting spiritual forces that want to withstand the advance of the Kingdom of God. We're fighting against the ills of society that have found their way into the lives of our parishioners. We're fighting the same fight that any business does with personnel and organizational challenges.

The statistics of many clergy families are frightening enough to dissuade many young preachers from joining the ministry. Discouragement, stress, loneliness, and fatigue top the charts of descriptive issues of the average pastor's family in America. There's endless pressure to be there for the needs of hurting people. There are personal expectations to represent Jesus well. There's the naked feeling of fishbowl living.

Why then do we do it? Why embrace the challenge? It's certainly not for fame. It's not for natural riches. Why do we pay this kind of a price? We do it because we're called. And we want to stand as bastions of defense against a society that is in a moral free fall. We own the vision.

So do you.

You wouldn't be in your current ministry assignment if you were only in it for love of self. You wouldn't be striving to build a godly company that provides jobs for families and pours wealth into the advancement of His Kingdom if you were just hoping for a fat 401k.

Of course we want to prosper. God didn't call us to poverty. He called us to be a blessing. Even so, our motivation for what we do is not merely to receive but to give. We're giving our lives for a higher cause.

We're owners.

Owning the vision will have positive effects. Here are a few examples:

First, it will bring security to your senior leader. It's important in serving your senior leader to know that he really does carry a heavier weight than anyone else. You and I may handle the bulk of the details and the tough personnel issues, but the buck stops with him. It's a great assurance for a senior leader to know that he's not alone in the harness.

The principle of synergy states that two individual parts, when combined, can achieve more than the sum of their individual parts. Even world class CEOs need to experience synergy. Even nationally known ministry leaders need the synergistic strength of toiling alongside a committed right-hand man. This dynamic brings security to the leader. Knowing that they're not alone during the sleepless nights of prayer and desperation brings great peace.

Second, it will bring healing to the leader. As you well know, it is impossible to lead without experiencing frequent criticism. Sometimes I think people must mistake me for a pin cushion. There must be something about leaders that inspires people to throw darts and arrows. We all face criticism. It's a byproduct of stepping up to the plate.

If we, as second-in-command leaders, experience criticism, our senior leaders do far more. If we own the vision with them, we'll face the criticism together and that will strengthen their heart.

Third, it will alleviate concern over the details. If I truly carry my leader's vision as my own, I will have a twofold motivation for carrying it with excellence. I'll want to please him and I'll also want to please myself. I'll want him to look good, but I will want to look good too.

My senior leader has a high level of excellence, but so do I. I want to guard his reputation in every area. The more I guard his, the more I guard mine too. I'm not just an employee. Our ministry is a reflection of who I am. It's not the source of my identity (that comes from my Father), but it *is* an expression of it.

One of the greatest compliments paid to Joseph in Scripture came when it was said that none of his senior leaders (Potiphar, the jail keeper, or Pharaoh) concerned themselves with anything under Joseph's care. When Joseph was in charge, his leaders were at peace.

Fourth, it lightens his load. I know this is a terribly obvious point, but it is still worth mentioning. Heavy burdens lie on the shoulders of the senior leader. Having a like-minded associate can lift the weight of the world.

Titus did this for Paul. In Second Corinthians 8, Paul made a couple of wonderful comments about Titus. He said that Titus had the same "earnestness" of care for the Corinthians that Paul did. It's one thing for an employer to have an employee who does a good job. It's quite another to have one who possesses the same earnest care as him. It's a rare but wonderful thing to know that your associate holds your burden and passion as his own.

Paul also said that Titus was his "partner." The literal definition of this word *partner* is to share in a mission. Paul's mission was Titus' mission. Titus' was Paul's. Paul was carrying the mandate to penetrate new nations with the gospel of Jesus Christ. Fortunately for him and all of us today, he wasn't carrying it alone. Titus was strapped to the vision too.

Fifth, it will free the leader to dream. If my leader knows that I'm implementing his vision as dutifully as if it were mine (since it *is* mine), he'll be free to dream. His job is to hear from God for the direction of the organization. He doesn't need to be concerned over the daily operations.

Not only does being an owner serve to strengthen the organization and the senior leader, but it will also provide specific benefits for *you.* Let me list several benefits to the right-hand man who truly owns the vision.

Favor. The assistant who truly carries his leader's heart will reap favor. This favor will come from both the senior leader and the people you serve. Your people know if you're an owner or a hireling. Jesus said in John 10 that His sheep will not follow the voice of a hireling.

Increased authority. An owner is a boss. Those who own a piece of the company have authority in the company.

The pleasure of God. An ownership mentality is in alignment with Paul's exhortation to approach all that we do for the approval and glory of God. Owners get to carry a piece of God's heart. I'm not convinced that He will share much of His burden with someone who is just living for payday. He likes to climb mountains with Moses. He likes to visit Joshuas who remain in the tent of meeting after everyone else is gone.

I want to please Him. I want God to smile on my ministry. Do you know that He smiles through our leaders? When we serve them, we're really serving God. When we serve our people, we're really serving Jesus.

Let me conclude with one of my favorite quotes from Dr. Martin Luther King Jr:

> What I'm saying to you this morning, my friends, is that even if it falls your lot to be a street sweeper, go on out and sweep streets like Michelangelo painted pictures; sweep streets like Handel and Beethoven composed music; sweep streets like Shakespeare wrote poetry; sweep streets so well that all the hosts of heaven and earth will have to pause and say, "Here lived a great street sweeper who swept his job well."

I want the "well done" of Heaven more than anything else. Don't you? Is it realistic for us to think that we'll get it from Heaven if we haven't first received it from those He has assigned for us to serve here on earth?

Own the vision!

If I advance, follow me! If I retreat, kill me! If I die, avenge me!

-Francois De La Rochefoucauld

Powerful indeed is the empire of habit.

-Publilius Syrus

Entrepreneurs are the forgotten heroes of America.

-Ronald Reagan

chapter ten

PROVERBS FOR THE RIGHT-HAND MAN

I will always be grateful for him. He changed my life in ways he will probably never know. What began as a chance encounter grew into a legendary friendship. (At least that's how I view it.) Let me tell you how I met him.

It was a hot, August morning in 1997 when he arrived to replace me as watchman. Our church was hosting a summer-long series of evangelistic meetings on the back of our property under a massive, circus-sized tent. Since all of our sound equipment had been carefully installed under the canvas canopy and was vulnerable to passersby, the men in our congregation had volunteered to stand watch around the clock.

I had volunteered for the 6:00 A.M. slot, and he came to relieve me at 9:00 A.M. Up to this point he and I were casual acquaintances at best, and I had no idea that he was obeying a prompting from the Lord to engage me in a friendship. I thought it was mere chance when we were scheduled for back-to-back guard duty. In hindsight I realize that God Himself must have arranged our schedules.

My most distinct memory of him was when he entered the tent with a massive biography of George Washington buried under one of his arms. I asked him if he frequently read biographies and his reply to my query became a core value in my development as a leader. He said, "Who could be better instructors in leadership than George Washington, Gandhi, Martin Luther King Jr., Teddy Roosevelt, Abe Lincoln, or Mother Theresa?" He went on to say, "Anyone called to leadership should become a student of the great leaders of our past. When you let the lives and principles of great leaders instruct and confront you, you will grow and develop in your own leadership ability."

I kept him company on his watch that day, and when I departed for home I felt that I had been visited by an angel. I sensed destiny hovering around our chance meeting. I was a better man and leader after one simple conversation. I found myself excited for our next shift of guard duty.

That was eight years ago. Since that initial encounter, he has assumed many roles in my life. He mentored me in business (I became his right-hand man in a start-up mortgage company); he was a stalwart friend in my darkest hour (he held me in his arms as I wept like a baby after the death of my first daughter); he has been one of my biggest cheerleaders, and he inspires me to this day.

He wrote to me recently, saying:

I perceive a subtle but widespread groundswell of believers who are looking past the traditional systems and are seeking to become living signs and wonders to their communities. All around me I am seeing evidence of a much more holistic style of Christian living, which appears to be trying to unite our lives, finances, and time to represent a total picture of what Christianity is supposed to be. I am seeing a de-emphasis of the mystical and a focus on a practical outworking of our faith in all areas. This includes business, education, and social reform issues. I am curious if you are seeing or sensing this yourself.

On a side note, I attended a powerful meeting last night. The focus of the meeting was to recognize and facilitate the exchange of wealth between Christian givers and the ministries that depend on their generosity. It's amazing to see the wonderful things that are happening all over our city to spread the message of Christ's love. It really got my mind turning and I'm excited to think about what lies ahead for a church that is committed to a lifestyle of generosity.

I always appreciate his observations and insights. Especially regarding business and leadership. His calling to business is just as strong as mine is to pastoring within a local church. He's added a lot to my life and leadership. Let me share some of the principles that he lives by and constantly challenges me to attain. I'll share them in proverbs style. Some principles will connect to the ones before or after them; others will seem more randomly placed. All of them will benefit the second-in-command leader.

Do not bring your leader problems. Bring them solutions. When confronted with a problem use your creativity and connections to come up with ideas to solve the problem.

Do not be afraid to contend in a positive way to persuade the mind of your leader. Good leaders welcome a healthy exchange of ideas and they respect well thought-out positions. In the end, you might need to lay your opinions aside and move forward with the decision of the leader; however, it is still a positive thing to dialogue and even disagree.

Be a greenhouse of ideas. Seed your mind continuously with ideas so that you will be able to bring creative, fresh concepts to your organization.

Shun the spotlight and pick up the toilet brush. If you are a person who is willing to deal with the tough, non-glorious problems that a leader has, you will create an aura around yourself of trust, dependability, and selflessness. This will carry you far.

Try new things. It is not sufficient to simply think of new ideas. You should be willing to move them to the next level. Learn how to take an idea from concept to implementation. Develop a system for birthing new ideas on a regular basis. It is likely that eight out of ten of them will fail. This is the burden of the leader. You must be prepared to fail in order to uncover new concepts and new pathways to success. Someone said, "It's not called failure—it's called education."

Don't just *buy into* the vision...customize it. Sure, your leader or your organization has a vision for what they are there to do, but you have to customize that vision to yourself. You have to find ways to make the vision work for you and the best way to do that is to match your gifts and talents up to it in the most efficient way possible.

Dress well. How do leaders dress? Like leaders. They dress as if they know where they are going. It's true that God looks at the heart, but we must still present a pleasant exterior.

Buy a day timer and learn how to use it. Ineffective time management has been the bane of many leaders.

Accept responsibility for failure. One of the fastest ways to lose credibility with your leader is to make excuses. They know that people fail, drop the ball, and get distracted. Accept responsibility, deal with the problems, and move on.

Don't dwell on your failures. Another quick way to lose credibility with your leader is to dwell on your failures and host a pity party. Failure is an INEVITABLE part of leadership. If your failures cripple you from trying new things or send you into a cocoon of self-evaluation, you should question your ability to be a leader. You must find healthy ways to cope with and move past failure. One of the most liberating quotes regarding failure came from President Theodore Roosevelt. He said:

> It is not the critic who counts, not the man who points out how the strong man stumbles or where the doer of deeds could have done better. The credit belongs to the man who is actually in the arena, whose face is marred by dust and sweat and blood, who strives valiantly, who errs and comes up short again and again, because there is no effort without error or shortcoming, but who knows the great enthusiasms, the great devotions, who spends himself for a worthy cause; who, at the best, knows, in the end, the triumph of high achievement, and who, at the worst, if he fails, at least he fails while daring greatly, so that his place shall never be with those cold and timid souls who knew neither victory nor defeat.

Keep up with the times. Take time to invest in learning new technologies that relate to successful organizations. Those business and church leaders who ignore the advances of technology are on a ride to cultural irrelevance and organizational stagnation. Technology is a significant part of our country and times. It represents a host of tools designed to enhance our ability to communicate. The efficiencies that these new tools bring into our lives are extraordinary. Any prospective team member should be willing to learn them.

Do not be afraid to ask for or seek promotions. I believe that one of the principles of Paul's letter to Timothy was that it is not only permissible, but desirable, to seek to be a leader. Organizations are desperate to find skilled, committed, and loyal leaders. Do not be afraid of letting your pride overtake you. Trust God to determine whether or not you get the promotion, but plant the seed of opportunity by applying for any leadership position you have a desire (and time) for.

Develop yourself as a communicator. Invest the time to read a broad range of books, listen to books and lectures on tape, and volunteer to communicate in any way that becomes available. Develop your communication skills in every media you can think of: written, electronic, spoken, etc.

Learn to keep a secret. Confidentiality breeds credibility. This point cannot be over-emphasized. If you lose the trust of your people, your leadership is lost. Someone once said, "Loose lips sink ships." The fastest way to lose credibility with those you lead is to betray confidence. It's important to remember that confidence is not gained simply by promising not to tell. It is gained by keeping *everyone's* confidence. You don't have to betray a person directly to lose their trust—just betray *other people's confidence* to them and they'll assume you'll do the same to them.

Learn to relate to your senior leader's spouse. The relationship between the right-hand man and his senior leader's spouse may be one of the most delicate relationships he will have. It requires a combination of great love and respect with huge doses of open and honest communication.

How should you relate to your senior leader's spouse? What are the boundary lines in your relationship? When should *they* defer to *you*? When should *you* defer *them*? These are tough but very relevant questions and they *must* be openly and freely discussed.

Let me offer a couple of pointers that will help to protect the relationship between the right-hand man and the senior leader's spouse.

The spouse must be honored. They are leaders in their own right and they carry a great weight of responsibility and ownership of the vision. They should be honored for their relational status as the senior leader's spouse and they should also be honored for their own giftedness and anointing. They will have a wisdom and perspective that is very necessary for the organization. Recognize and embrace this.

There must be a clarification of the role of the spouse. Although they should be honored as a leader, keep in mind that a lack of clarification of their authority and responsibility can create confusion. Any ambiguity in role, responsibility, or authority can be confusing for the staff members who attempt to adhere to the established flow-charts of authority.

The spouse must be in the loop of communication. It is incumbent on senior leaders to communicate the vision—and the decisions of implementation surrounding it—with their spouses. It is a very awkward, uncomfortable thing if a spouse is left out of significant decisions.

Maintain proper boundaries. Although a great friendship may develop between you and your senior leaders, it is appropriate to maintain respect and propriety in the relationship—especially with your leader's spouse.

If any of these areas need adjustment, communicate openly and honestly about them. The following are some practical ground rules that apply to communication in general but that are especially vital in your relating with your senior leader's spouse.

1. **Remember that the relationship is more important than the issue.** If God sent you to work with your leaders, the issue should take a back seat to the relationship. Of course if it is an issue of conscience or morality, it must be resolved satisfactorily, but if it is an issue of style or preference or opinion, it should never take precedence over the relationship.

2. **If you need to confront, do it with a humble, appealing manner.** Paul told Timothy to never rebuke an elder but to entreat him as a father. Although in many ways you are a peer with your leaders, don't approach confrontation from a peer level. Approach it with the respectful heart of an appeal.

3. **Use non-offensive terminology.** Any time you can avoid phrases that elicit defensive responses you will be ahead of the game. Phrases like "you always do this" or "you make me feel like" will get you nowhere. No one *always* does a particular action. Few people *intentionally* set out to make someone else feel bad. If you need to address issues of personal conflict, say something like: "I was a little confused when you said this or did that." This gives them the opportunity to share their heart and motives without feeling attacked. When they clarify their intentions, you can then say, "Thank you for clarifying things for me. Without knowing your heart, I was beginning to feel hurt" (or frustrated or whatever the emotion might have been).

4. **Allow them to respond in turn.** We all have blind spots. If we're identifying a blind spot in someone else, there is probably a high likelihood that we have one too. Sometimes I've been shocked because I have pressed for discussion and an opportunity to express to someone how I had been feeling only to discover that *they* had been feeling hurt by *me*. When confronted, humility says, "Thank you. Tell me more."

5. **Establish a peaceful course of action.** In a setting of trust, love, and mutual respect, it is easy to walk out the commitments that lead to health and relationship.

I want to conclude this chapter by looking at one more "proverb."

Learn to relate to visionary leaders. Many senior leaders are *visionary leaders* who possess a unique mixture of strengths and weaknesses that serve to make them both powerfully effective in their calling as well as very challenging to work with.

A *visionary leader* is defined as the head of a group or organization who has been entrusted with the vision for that group; this is often a father figure, mentor, or one standing in an apostolic role. The following outline (taken with permission from a teaching by Michael Sullivant from the Metro Vineyard Fellowship in Kansas City) provides great insight for working alongside these visionary leaders that can be helpful in strengthening relationships with them.

1. Determine whether or not God has called you to work with a particular visionary leader and to support his or her vision. This is the basic and most important question. Of course, a major part of this decision is determined by whether or not the visionary leader is a righteous person. Another basic factor: discerning if he wants you and trusts you as a partner.

2. One of the characteristics of God's visionary leaders is that they have extraordinary confidence in their judgment and their ability to lead. Although this is a genuine gifting from God, this dynamic can make them more susceptible to arrogance, so they need prayer in this area.

3. Visionary leaders often initiate in many areas with others who have different gifts and capacities. This often causes them not to be able to think about the totality of the expanding work. This is exacerbated by the tendency we all have to act as if the whole work is that particular part of the work that is most important to us.

4. These visionary leaders also often experience loneliness in their work and vision because...

   a. Their confidence leaves others with the impression that they do not need anyone else.

   b. Their vision allows them to see ahead of others; so, in things most important to them, rarely does someone else's vision totally encompass theirs. The gap between their vision and that of others is where they often stand alone.

   c. They are typically not good at functioning as partners. They are warm and affirming when they are recruiting, but often less so with those who have signed on for the long haul. The recruited person comes to feel demoted [once he/she is onboard], while the leader thinks he is affirming the person's maturity and value simply by allowing the new person to assume his or her role on the team. In addition, the confidence that visionary leaders have in their own judgment can make it difficult for them to hear the Lord through others. They *want* others to be partners, but often the press of the vision, and the many decisions that go along with it, mean there is not enough time to bring others in as the "party of the first part," even though this may be a sincere desire. In some instances they want partnership in implementing the work but not in making the decisions about what should be done.

   d. In the nature of their visionary work, they relate to greater numbers of people than most. This is a prime example of the principle that "The man with many friends comes to a ruin." Relationally, they often get spread out and overcommitted.

   e. Because many people want to be close to them for selfish reasons, and they have often been burned in relationships before, they hold people at a safe distance. (This is sometimes the reaping of what they have sown, in that they have also drawn close to people for the sake of their own vision.) There is a pressure to be relationally utilitarian.

 f. There can be a high turnover rate of subordinates who did not understand or tolerate these dynamics.

5. How do I relate to these gifted leaders?

 a. Pray for them, especially when you are involved in a project with them.

 b. Support wholeheartedly all that you hold in agreement with them.

 c. When you have questions that leave you unsure, assume the best and trust their gift of vision.

 d. When you think they may be misled, direct confrontation is really the best approach. Since their God-given confidence can make it difficult to present differing points of view, try asking questions about issues as a helpful way to move into discussions.

 e. Encourage them to have contacts with other peer ministers and visionaries who can challenge and stimulate their thinking in ways that others cannot.

 f. Encourage them to value the gift of others rather than seeing the Body of Christ only as people who can be employed in their vision.

 g. Walk with the Lord and be a part of a team so you do not "need" the approval or blessing of the visionary leaders. Having others in your life can meet some of your need for equal partnership.

 h. Make it a goal to consistently affirm these leaders because they need encouragement more than they appear to.

 i. Be loyal! Guard against disloyal comments to others, especially to those who (for right or wrong reasons) have a grievance. Be careful when you "defend" them so as not to uncover the weaknesses you see so clearly, and thus defame their character. One way to deal with situations that arise is to agree with legitimate criticisms and show the criticizer how to cope, rather than denying that the visionary leader has a weakness.

j.   Write your thoughts, concerns, or thanks briefly, rather than initiating conversations. This can be an effective way to keep your "relational fire" burning.

k.   Ask for appointments when you need them; they [the senior leader] will probably not take initiative with the low-maintenance long-termers.

l.   Don't expect a lot of socializing (or hang time) with them. Their low need for this does not seem normal! Their vision is their entertainment.

m.   Pressure them to take vacations. They will be grateful you did.

n.   Protect them from administrative details. Encourage them to delegate.

o.   Don't expect appreciation from them for figuring all this out!

He who has never learned to obey cannot be a good commander.

-Aristotle

There is no worse mistake in public leadership than to hold out false hope soon to be swept away.

-Sir Winston Leonard Spencer Churchill

Every man who takes office…either grows or swells, and when I give a man an office, I watch him carefully to see whether he is swelling or growing.

-Thomas Woodrow Wilson

I KISSED HIM!

I couldn't believe I had done it. Where had I gone wrong? When did deception enter my heart? Sure, I had been struggling for a while, but my concerns were very valid. I knew we needed to work some things out, but how could I have kissed him? I'm no Judas. I'm loyal. How could I have been found holding the knife?

✦✦✦✦✦

I'm afraid we have to do it. We have to examine the topics of loyalty and betrayal. We can't escape them. They are crucial for a study of the servant-leader.

I have felt the sting of offense pierce my heart on numerous occasions. I have even toyed with the tantalizing temptation to disloyalty. Of course, I never planned to do it. I didn't set out to develop a bad attitude toward my boss. It usually starts innocently. I believe that very few people set out to betray. I know that Judas didn't.

Judas believed Jesus was the Messiah. He intended to follow Him to the end. He wasn't a traitor at heart. In fact, Judas was fiercely loyal. He was a man of passion.

He was a member of the zealot party, the intensely devout religious group that longed to see the Kingdom of God established to overthrow the oppressive Roman regime in Jerusalem.

Jesus chose Judas to be His disciple. Remember, Jesus did nothing randomly or arbitrarily. He was a man of purpose and intentionality. He prayed all night before selecting the 12 who would be ordained to be with Him. He wanted Judas. He saw something of a zealous warrior in his soul and He wanted him on His team. In fact, Jesus trusted him enough to commission him to serve as the treasurer for the ministry.

We all know that financial decisions are reserved for the most trusted confidants. The newest employee of an organization is not usually privy to the salaries of the senior staff or the budgets of the various departments. Those facts are reserved for those who truly need to know and can be trusted with the information. Jesus trusted Judas with the finances of His ministry, and His trust was not ill-founded. He didn't choose a con man in the hopes of rehabilitating him. He saw greatness in Judas.

How then did Judas end up holding the knife? How was it that his lips bore the kiss of betrayal during the darkest night of Jesus' ministry? What happened?

The answer is very frightening because none of us are immune to it. You see, *Judas was betrayed first.* His own expectations betrayed him.

As a member of the zealot party, he was confident that Jesus had come to overthrow the Roman government. He didn't expect Jesus to surrender to the Romans. He expected fire from Heaven to ignite the Roman crosses that littered the ditches of the Jerusalem roadways. He didn't expect his salvation to expire and die on one.

Judas was not a betrayer at heart. He would never have dreamed that a disappointing revelation would begin a chain of events that would eventually lead him into a covenant with the enemy.

Betrayal begins in our hearts when our expectations betray us.

Beware of *dis*appointment. If we break the word down, we see an appointment with a negative clinging to it. Judas' expectation turned bitter and he began looking for 30 pieces of silver with which to betray Jesus.

Judas is probably the most famous traitor in history. There was another case of betrayal in Scripture, though, that warrants an evaluation too. This case involves a father and a son. The father's name was David. The son's was Absalom.

Please journey with me several centuries into our past and observe their relational dynamics. We can learn some insights from this father and son that might save our ministry. Our tour guide is speaking.

✦✦✦✦✦

"King David is in the palace. We haven't seen much of him lately. I'm sure he's very busy with the demands of the kingdom. He's built quite a name for himself. The people love him. Israel is feared by the nations of the world.

"Do you remember his resumé? His career started when he liberated Israel from the fear of Goliath. No one has forgotten that. He was a legend before he was 20 years old. Then he became a prince when he married Saul's daughter. Of course, in order to marry her, David was required to pay a gruesome dowry of 100 foreskins of Philistine warriors. It was here that his heart was truly seen because instead of doing the required minimum for his bride-to-be, David risked his life and brought her father *200* foreskins.

"He rose to such prominence through his military exploits that the maidens of the land swooned as they sang, 'David has slain his ten thousands!' He was the ultimate warrior-king. He conquered nation after nation. He wasn't afraid to personally lead the troops into battle, and the people have always been secure with him as their king.

"There is another aspect to his greatness, though. He's not just a valiant warrior—he's also a deeply spiritual man. In fact, he has restored national pride and commitment to the God of our fathers. It was he, not Saul, who sought out the Ark of the Covenant so the manifest glory of God could be seen in our midst again. He's currently storing up the materials for a permanent temple for our God. We truly love him.

"However...we haven't seen much of him lately. I'm sure he's very busy.

"We *do* see Absalom, though. In fact, he's standing right over there. What a handsome man! He's the real deal. Someone with his looks and station in life would usually be aloof and withdrawn, but not Absalom. He's at the city gate nearly every day.

"I think his greatest gift is exhortation. He's encouraged me personally on several occasions. I'm shocked that he even remembered my name. I love David, but I'm sure glad that Absalom is around to help him."

◆◆◆◆◆

Were we to fast-forward a couple of months we would see a very different sight. We wouldn't see the humbly smiling Absalom encouraging the people at the gates. We would see him proudly entering the tent of his father's concubines. We would see him moving his own furniture into the king's palace. We would see anarchy.

Where is David? Has he already transitioned the reins of the kingdom to Absalom? Does he know that Absalom is sleeping with his wives? Is he here? Is he dead? Oh, I see him now.

He's fleeing! He's barefoot and his head is bowed as he and his closest supporters depart the city. His mighty men want to fight, but he's ordered them to run. What on earth has happened?

It's very simple really. Absalom betrayed him.

It doesn't make sense! Why would a son betray his father? As with Judas, the answer is very simple—and frightening.

Absalom got hurt. David hurt him. It started many years ago.

The unthinkable had happened. Absalom's brother, Amnon, fell in love with his half-sister, Tamar, and in an angry moment of lust, he raped her and then banned her from his presence. Word of the crime reached their father's ears, and then the unthinkable happened again.

David did nothing.

No one knew what he was thinking. He was such a righteous man that it just didn't make sense—especially for Absalom. He felt betrayed by David. His father should have been there in agreement with his anger. He certainly should have been there for his own daughter.

The seeds of betrayal were sown deep inside the furrow of Absalom's wound. Was he justified in his anger? Of course he was. Was he more righteous than David in his indignation? Absolutely. However, he didn't realize that the devil is a sower too.

It's not just God who sows. Jesus told us that He delights to sow the good seed of His word into our hearts, but He also told us that satan sows too. He sows thistle seeds along with the fruit seeds. He sows tares in and among the wheat. He is there to sow seeds of betrayal when wounds have plowed the soil of our hearts.

He got to Absalom. If we're not careful, he can get to us too.

Well, Absalom got his revenge. He had Amnon murdered, and later had his father David sprinting from the city. Unfortunately, *betrayal always ends in death*. The final glimpse of Judas was him hanging from a tree (that is until the rope broke and he fell into a bloody heap on the ground of the potter's field).

In *his* final portrait, Absalom was not enjoying his newly won kingdom. He was hanging from a tree. His beautiful, long hair acted as a noose, and three spears protruded from his side. He had been killed by Joab—another betrayer at heart.

Don't you feel uplifted now? Aren't you a little more inspired to serve as a leader after these stories? We will be if we learn. There are several insights that this gruesome tale affords us.

First, it is imperative that senior leaders address the issues of their kingdom. It should never be left to sons to deal with their father's issues. The son isn't graced for it. *David* should have dealt with Amnon (according to the law of their day). His failure to act cost him *two* sons.

If your senior leader fails to address problems in your organization, he sets you up for a dangerous fall. He needs to address and resolve the delicate issues. I'm not saying that you aren't wise enough or skilled enough to navigate the challenges and bring a healthy resolve to them. I'm saying that if he refuses to face them, he risks setting you up for offense and losing the faith of the people.

I realize that this might be a confusing point, since part of your job is to help your senior leader. You probably handle a hundred awkward moments and situations every year on his behalf. Most of that is probably appropriate and necessary.

I never ask my senior leader to do my job for me. I'm not afraid to step up and tackle the challenging situations. However, the issue isn't about my ability to resolve conflict as much as it is about finding the healthiest way to resolve that conflict. Sometimes the people need to hear from him. Sometimes the word and wisdom of the right-hand man isn't enough.

Let me offer a few guidelines to help you know when the situation mandates the involvement of the senior leader. I believe the senior leader should be involved if the matter includes any of the following:

1.   Conflict with a significant leader in the organization.

2.   Significant disciplinary action.

3.   Decisions that will affect the course of direction for the company.

4.   Parties who have a lengthy history of relationship with the senior leader.

5.   Major relational disputes among the senior staff.

These guidelines certainly aren't all-inclusive and they will require some discussion and clarification between you and your senior leader. The point is simply that there are certain situations that should only be handled by the senior leader (or at least with his input). Talk about these parameters of authority. Ask the question: "What can I handle on my own and what do you want to have a voice in?" Discussion in advance can spare Absalom's confusion later on.

Second, if senior leaders fail to address an issue, it is incumbent on the second in command to challenge the senior leader. David failed to discipline Amnon, but Absalom didn't have to betray David because of it—rather, he could have challenged him. A careful study of this biblical account shows us that Absalom bit his tongue and allowed the hurt to turn bitter. Who knows how history might have been different had he courageously spoken up. Perhaps we would have a record of Absalom's Temple instead of Solomon's Temple.

Is it intimidating at times to confront your senior leader? Of course it is! It shouldn't be necessary to do it very often, though. If you're constantly confronting your senior leader, either you are out of line or your senior leader isn't leading. If it is the latter, you may want to ask the Lord if you should still be following him.

Let me suggest a few pointers on how to challenge your leader:

1. **Appeal—don't confront.** Paul exhorted Timothy to entreat an elder as a father versus delivering a sound rebuke. How do you appeal? You boldly present your case from a posture of humility and respect. The Lord didn't assign you to your leader to change him; however, there *will* be times when decisions or attitudes need to be challenged.

2. **Appeal in private.** I once heard someone say that "Loyalty in public yields leverage in private." Your leader should never fear that you might challenge him in front of the staff or the parishioners or the customers. He needs to know that you have his back. If you need to challenge him, do it, but do it in private.

3. **Don't accuse or attack.** Couch your appeal in the form of a question. Ask him to explain why he did or said things the way he did. Tell him, "I was a little confused when you said that, because it came across like...." A blunt rebuke doesn't go very far with anyone-let alone your boss.

4. **Use the term "we" versus "you."** Instead of saying, "I think you handled that poorly in there" or "I totally disagree with you on this one," use terms like "I was a little concerned by our last meeting" or "Let's process a little because I'm not sure that was handled quite right."

5. **If he holds fast to his decision, support him (unless his decision is unbiblical or unethical).** If he is not motivated by the principles of Scripture, then you must decide if God is calling you to remain at his side. There are some decisions you will disagree with from a practical, logistical standpoint. Those you can flex on. There are other decisions, however, that cross moral lines. Don't let your name be associated with those.

6. **If he defers to your suggestion, share the credit with him.** Don't share with the staff that you disagreed with him and that he came around to your way of thinking. Honor him.

7. **If he is unwilling to address the issue and you feel you have no choice but to leave, leave appropriately.** Many wounded leaders have failed to leave appropriately and, consequently, have left a wake of disillusioned, hurting followers behind them. Let me comment on this delicate point by quoting from Gene Edwards's book, *A Tale of Three Kings*.[1] In this classic story on biblical authority, Edwards aptly writes about the only appropriate way to leave a Kingdom after all biblical options for restoration and resolve have been tried but to no avail:

> How does a person know when it is finally time to leave the Lord's anointed...?
>
> David never made that decision. The Lord's anointed made it for him. The king's own decree settled the matter...
>
> Only then did David leave. No, he fled. Even then, he never spoke a word or lifted a hand against Saul. And please note this: David did not split the kingdom when he made his departure. He did not take part of the population with him. He left alone.
>
> Alone. *All* alone. King Saul II never does that. He always takes those who "insist on coming along."
>
>> Yes, people do insist on going with you, don't they?
>>
>> They are willing to help you found the Kingdom of King Saul II.
>>
>> Such men never dare leave alone.

---

1. Gene Edwards, *A Tale of Three Kings* (Wheaton, IL: Tyndale House Publishers, Inc., 1980, 1992), pp. 27-28.

But David left alone. You see, the Lord's true anointed can leave alone. There's only one way to leave a kingdom:

Alone.

All alone."

What I'm offering here is not a coaching on office politics. What I'm presenting is the heart of a loyal supporter. When Joab conquered the city of Rabbah, he contacted David and said, "You'd better get over here and march through the city first or else the people will give me the credit for this victory." That's the heart of a right-hand man. It was Joab who had achieved the victory, but he knew that he needed to keep the loyalty of the people firmly attached to David.

Third, unresolved hurt is a fast track toward offense. It wasn't Absalom's fault that Amnon raped his sister. It wasn't his fault that David failed to respond. Absalom was justified in his outrage. His problem was that he kept his wound concealed—at least for a little while.

It was exposed when he stood at the gate soliciting the favor of the citizens.

Fourth, be careful with your encouragement. Absalom stole the hearts of the people of Israel when he encouraged them at the gate. Encouragement is powerful because it always strengthens decisions and resolve. While David was absent, Absalom encouraged the unrest in the hearts of the people. The result: the people transferred their loyalty from a godly, selfless leader into the hands of an encouraging young man who had done nothing of any honorable significance.

In the following chapter, we will explore some more of the practical landmarks of the disloyal spirit as well as the dynamics of healthy encouragement. Part of your role as the second in command is to keep your finger on the pulse of your people. How do you encourage them if their hurts and complaints are leveled at David? How do you respond if they dreamily sigh, "If only you were in charge"? Many an Absalom have hung from the branches of a tree because they failed this test.

That is not our destiny!

Learn to obey before you command.

-Solon

What a curious phenomenon it is that you can get men to die for the liberty of the world that will not make the little sacrifice that is needed to free themselves from their own individual bondage.

-Bruce Barton

One of the true tests of leadership is the ability to recognize a problem before it becomes an emergency.

-Arnold Glasow

IF ONLY *YOU* WERE IN CHARGE!

I just don't get it. Absalom was *never* known for performing noble exploits. He built a statue *in his own honor*. He had his brother murdered. He was vain. In fact, it was a public event whenever he would cut his hair. He wasn't a God-worshiper. How could he have stolen the hearts of the people from David? How could they have left their righteous leader to follow his arrogant son? What did Absalom do that elicited such a following from people?

The answer is very simple. He encouraged them.

Is that all? Isn't that a good thing?

Sometimes.

Before we dissect the dynamics of healthy encouragement, let me point out the obvious. Most every organization has someone involved with it who is discontented and unhappy. There are no perfect businesses and there are no perfect churches. No matter how wonderful you are as a leader someone will find your flaw. I don't say that with any conscious cynicism. It's simply the truth. Some people will get hurt, and they will get hurt while involved with you and me. Acknowledging that does not excuse hurtful behavior on the part of any leaders, and it certainly doesn't minimize the feelings of those who are hurt. It just brings a clarifying perspective.

I was a little surprised to discover that not everyone in our church thought I hung the moon. I don't say that out of pride. I say it out of the common mind-set of leaders: We judge ourselves by our motives. Others judge us by our actions. I *never* mean to hurt anyone, but sadly, it does happen sometimes.

I have a pastor's heart and I want everyone in our church to connect and form relationships and receive meaningful ministry. Unfortunately, there are some people who visit our church and never want to return. You don't have to look very hard to find someone who has been disappointed or disillusioned in any ministry or organization.

Here's the challenge: These disappointed souls often find their way into the office of the second in command. If not skillfully handled, the encouragement provided there can become deadly.

Here's how it happened with me.

Like Judas and Absalom before me, I never intended to turn disloyal. I love my senior leader and I truly enjoy working with him. I wouldn't have staked my allegiance to him if I didn't believe that God's hand was on his life and that I was called to serve him. I sincerely believe that the Lord is grading me based on how faithfully I serve in my current position.

I don't have a problem communicating with my boss. He and I have a wonderful relationship. We relate on several fronts and we're both comfortable with each of them. We're colleagues. We're friends. We're co-laborers in ministry. We have an employer-employee relationship. It's great. There are no issues in any of these roles. How was it then, that I began sharpening my knife?

I think I was standing at the gate. By the way, that's a *good* place for a right-hand man to stand. It wasn't betrayal for Absalom to stand in the gate. That's where the people are.

A wonderful responsibility and blessing for the right-hand man is that they often have significant contact with the general assembly of people. That's important to me because I don't want to pastor from a distance. I want to know the people. I realize that as ministries and businesses grow, the emphasis of the senior staff must shift to strengthening the various leaders of the organization. The Jethro model (see Exod. 18) is still wise; however, there is always a need to know what is in the hearts of the individuals that comprise your organization.

That's what Absalom was doing. That's what I was doing. The problem is not in exploring the heart condition of the people. The problem begins when that exploration turns ugly, and, sadly, it often does.

I don't quite understand why ten compliments can be wiped out by one criticism. Ten families can join our church, and I'm still devastated by the one who leaves in offense. I'm not sure if that's a good pastor's heart or if it reveals a need for more security in me. All I know is that when the people express their frustrations or criticisms, it is a vulnerable time for an associate leader—especially when those criticisms are leveled at the senior leader.

First of all, they shouldn't be coming to you. Jesus said that if we have an issue with our brother or sister, we should go directly to them. He didn't say, "If you need to resolve conflict, go to your brother—unless your brother is also your senior leader. In that case, go to a different brother and get prayer or go to the associate leader and get wisdom." He said go to your brother. If people would do this, one of three things would happen:

1. The senior leader could share his heart and perspective, and healing and resolution would then occur.

2. The senior leader would eventually see a blind spot in his life and would receive an opportunity to change.

3. The people could leave with a clear conscience before God and without a wake of hurt behind them.

What I have found, far too often, is that rather than biblically approaching the senior leader, people come to me. It's probably equally true that if they have a concern with me they go to a different staff person.

I don't mean to come across as too insensitive toward people who feel that they need wisdom regarding the best course of action. On the other hand, there is grave danger that occurs when the course of action doesn't include direct communication between them and the involved brother.

Back to my story. I was sharpening my knife.

I had begun to develop a concern about a particular area in our church. I felt that it was an area that needed the attention of our senior pastor, so I began to consider the best way to approach him about it. As I was considering it, several people shared their frustration with me regarding the same issue. Their frustration fueled my own, and before I realized it, I was standing in the center of Absalom's crossroad. What would I do with their concerns?

Since I myself was frustrated and concerned, would I elicit their loyalty and support? Would I speak the language of Absalom, which says things like: "You're absolutely correct" and "I completely agree"? Would I tell them that "I'm concerned over those very issues" and "I've been praying about how to address those exact concerns"? Or would I respond like Jesus and say, "Go to your brother. If you're nervous, I will pray for courage. If you think you'll back down, I'll grab your hand right now and we will resolve this. One way or the other we will bring healing and restoration. None of us will walk around with the poison of offense flowing through our veins." Let me quickly clarify that having a concern doesn't mean that we're poisoned. We *will* have concerns at times; however, unresolved concern can turn to poison quite easily.

Absalom's style of speaking never promotes confrontation and subsequent healing. It simply encourages the concerned person's point of view. My agreeing with someone's concern and leaving it at that does nothing more than justify their frustration in their own mind. It doesn't serve to promote a resolution of the problem. Before we offer blanket encouragement of someone's concerns we should ask them:

1. Have you gone to this person to try to resolve this?

2. Do you know all of the facts?

3.   Do you know what the other party was thinking?

4.   Have you spoken with anyone else about this?

5.   What does the Bible say you should do in this situation?

6.   Before you offer them any counsel, remember that Proverbs 18:17 says, "*The first to plead his case seems right.*"

These questions apply regarding any area of hurt or frustration, but they are especially important if the concern is directed toward the senior leader. I wish I had remembered to practice them. Instead, I allowed my frustration to build.

My frustrations were valid. In reality, though, they were probably only about a four on the scale of one to ten in severity. A four is still valid, but somehow it quickly grew. With each person who shared the same concern, I began to wonder if my concerns were really a five or a six. I should have known better. I should have run into his office and said, "Help me process what's happening in my heart." Instead, I began to watch for further instances.

Sure enough, I saw them. I think we always see certain problems when we look for them. Each time I saw them I grew more concerned. Each time someone shared their concern, I grew a little more indignant *and* a little more encouraging.

Before long, my little level-four frustrations had become unbearable. I had gone from being a little bit concerned to genuinely hurt. I had gone from thinking we needed to tweak some of our procedures to thinking our ship was sinking.

Eventually, I couldn't bear it. Someone had to speak up. Someone had to lead.

So I called him. And I unloaded.

I'm so embarrassed about it now. My concern really was valid, but it was still only a four on a scale of one to ten. The bigger problem was that my Absalom attitude was now a seven or an eight. How had I become offended? Where did it begin?

I think it started when I didn't share my initial concern with him. I think it was compounded the first time I listened to someone confirm my concern. After that, it was all downhill. Every observation of the perceived problem was fuel to the fire until it grew from something that simply needed adjusting to something I thought was a true injustice.

Had I addressed my concerns initially, three things would have happened:

1. He would have taken ownership where necessary.

2. He would have shared some wisdom that wasn't available to me in my current position.

3. We would have fixed the problem.

As it happened, we did fix the problem, but we also caused some damage in the process.

Let me list the progressive steps of disloyalty without the narrative. Disloyalty usually follows this pattern:

1. A wound occurs.

2. The wound is not discussed.

3. A sense of injustice develops.

4. Others (whether innocently or intentionally) confirm the sense of injustice.

5. We become keenly aware of similar injustices.

6. We feel the need to champion the cause of these injustices.

7. We blame the leader for the injustice (without having given them the opportunity to make it right).

8. We grow resentful.

9. We feel justified in receiving the loyalty of others.

10. We begin sharpening our knife.

Betrayal always develops out of an offense, and offenses are always birthed out of a wound. Therefore, the surest way to remain free from the spirit of Absalom is to immediately resolve all hurts. You *will* get hurt. Your senior leader will hurt you. Go to him! Appeal to him! Share your heart! Cry! Take ownership for any part that you may have handled poorly. Extend grace. Forgive so you can be forgiven.

Remember, the devil has you in his sights. If he can get you to fall, he'll damage your senior leader. Don't make the mistake of thinking you're not a target. You're one of the biggest targets in your organization. Surprisingly, he targets you through the confessions of the people you serve.

I certainly hope it doesn't sound like I think the average church member or business employee has a bad attitude. I absolutely do not. What I've found though is that I'm just not strong enough to absorb their hurts and concerns.

Neither are you.

I can't listen to someone's offense without eventually getting stained by it. That's the nature of bitterness—it defiles. To be faithful to my calling and my leaders, I must be an agent of resolution. I must direct them to the Lord and their offending brother. Anything beyond that puts me in Absalom's crossroad.

When hurt by my leader I have no alternative but to share my heart with him. Sure, it might be difficult and it might get a little ugly before it gets fully resolved, but I'd rather face the gore of confrontation than the gore of my own innards spilling on the ground of the potter's field.

As the second in command, you will experience conflict with your leader and you will also be the sounding board for the hurts and concerns of your people. Remember, darts stick; they don't bounce. The darts of offense will be thrown and they will sometimes stick. It's okay if they hit you, but you must get them out immediately.

This is one of the greatest tests you will face, but Jesus wouldn't have allowed you to face it unless He was confident that you would pass. When He looks at you, He doesn't see an Absalom.

He sees a David.

We were always dreaming of how it was going to be.

-George Lucas

I don't dream at night, I dream all day; I dream for a living.

-Steven Spielberg

Happy are those who dream dreams and are willing to pay the price to make them come true.

-Anonymous

Dream no small dreams for they have no power to move the hearts of men.

-Goethe

The future belongs to those who believe in the beauty of their dreams.

-Eleanor Roosevelt

It takes a lot of courage to show your dreams to someone else.

-Erma Bombeck

TELL ME YOUR DREAMS

"Nothing happens until someone starts to dream!"

"Let your dreams carry you to the front door of the impossible!" "Live your life in such a way that you're absolutely bound to fail if God doesn't show up!"

"What would you risk for God if you knew you *couldn't* fail?"

I was eating it up. My pastor was preaching on the common denominators of organizations that grow. He said this about successful individuals or corporations:

1.   God uses the person who has a dream.

2.   God uses the person who expects their organization to grow.

3.   God uses the person who is willing to risk failure.

4.   God uses the person who doesn't know how to quit.

This particular sermon marked me. I determined from that moment on that I would dream big for God. I determined to live and act like God really is big and on my side.

This sermon was the conclusion of a wonderful series entitled "Building Unshakeable People in Shakeable Times." It was one of my favorite studies in the Bible—an evaluation of the life of Joseph. He was the perfect picture of a successful right-hand man. He possessed great leadership skill, the ability to dream, and impeccable character. He rose to the second highest rank in the most powerful nation of his day without ever once compromising his integrity. His life teaches us that if we stand firm on a strong bed of character while simultaneously dreaming as high as the stars, the Lord will promote us until our leaders trust us fully and even Pharaoh calls us "father."

He didn't always have this strength of character. It was beaten into him. I imagine yours didn't come to you easily either. It never does. Great character is not formed in a college classroom—it's birthed alone in the dark during the crucible times of life. That's where leadership is born, too. Let's look at Joseph's story for a few minutes from a leadership perspective.

Joseph was a dreamer who possessed a very special gift. In fact, it's probably the most important gift that a leader can possess. He had the ability to interpret and release the dreams of others.

"Behold the dreamer!" That's what his brothers said when Joseph approached them from a distance. The colorful coat of their father's love hung loosely around his muscular, young frame, and they could still hear his boastful words: *"I have dreamed a dream!"* Little did they know that before the night was out, they would betray him, contemplate his murder, and ultimately sell him into slavery where he would die a thousand deaths and then be promoted as one of the most powerful men in the most powerful nation of their day. Little did they know that they would one day beg for bread from his hand. They scoffed, *"Behold the dreamer!"*

Joseph dreamed a dream that his family would bow down before him—and he awoke on the back of an Ishmaelite camel on his way to a nightmarish season of pain, suffering, and *favor* beyond his wildest dreams.

That's the way it is with dreamers. God uses the dream to test and refine the dreamer so that their character can withstand the pressure that will accompany the fulfillment of the dream.

The jealousy of his brothers landed Joseph as a slave in Egypt in the household of Potiphar, Pharaoh's chief executioner.

It was there, in a foreign, fearful place, that Joseph displayed his greatness. He began to serve. The hand of the Lord was upon him, and he served Potiphar with such excellence and skill that the entire household prospered. He grew in strength and favor until Potiphar didn't even bother to concern himself with anything under his care. He trusted Joseph implicitly.

It was at this stage of his development that he faced the deadliest of attacks that are leveled against leaders. His moral purity came under fire.

Leaders, we *must* learn to live a lifestyle of purity! Our moral integrity is centered in our enemy's sights.

It's important to remember that strong leadership is attractive. Joseph was not only naturally handsome and well-built but he was also a strong leader. Decisiveness and strength of will are attractive character traits, and the enemy will attempt to exploit them.

Potiphar's wife became infatuated with him.

It happens to leaders constantly. I was with a man this week who is a godly husband and father, and yet he could see the hand of the enemy at work to derail his destiny. One of his employees had begun to aggressively pursue a sexual relationship with him, and he had to take the drastic step of removing her. It was a tough decision that invited the wrath of some of the other employees, but it brought Heaven to its feet in triumphant ovation.

Purity is power and the Lord is looking for men so empowered. These are the men whom He can promote.

Our society is in a moral free fall, and leaders are not exempt—they are actually at heightened risk. They carry tremendous pressure. They are responsible for the welfare of others, and the enemy would love nothing more than to take them out. When leaders indulge in moral sin, the fabric of society is weakened.

Joseph came close.

Potiphar's wife attempted everything from simple flirtation to outright seduction. When he refused to engage in an affair she suggested that they just spend time together. Time after time he rebuffed her advances but time after time she returned. She ignored his statement that this relationship would be a sin against his God and she continued with her advances.

When it became apparent to her that Joseph would not fall, her rejection became rage. She lied. She screamed. She framed him. She had him sentenced to a prison deeper than the empty well that his brothers had used when they sought to crush his dreams.

Remember that Potiphar was the chief executioner. If the chief hangman throws you into prison, the odds are that you're on death row. There was no help and no hope for Joseph. He was in hell. He was forgotten. He had nothing to live for...

...Except that *the Lord went with him into prison.* Somehow Joseph drew enough strength from the Lord to begin serving again. Rather than dying in a corner of his cell, Joseph became the right-hand man to the prison warden. As with Potiphar, the warden didn't bother to concern himself with anything that Joseph did. He, too, trusted him implicitly.

One morning he awoke and began his daily service of the prisoners when he noticed something. Two of the prisoners were sad. It's absurd to me that the Bible highlights the fact that two prisoners were sad. They were all sad! They were in prison—on death row. They were all miserable and desperate. How was it that Joseph noticed their pain? Once he noticed it, why did he care?

Incidentally, when the Scripture said that the men were *sad,* it used a word that means to experience such profound grief and sadness that the mourner's countenance is altered. Joseph didn't see two angry, sullen men. He saw two men whose sorrow was hurting them. And he reached out to them despite his own pain. He released the gift of encouragement there in the dark and he asked them, "*Why are you sad?*"

It was a risky question. Their response could have ruined Joseph. They said, "We have dreamed a dream."

Oh no! That's how it all began in the first place. All of the misery began when Joseph dreamed his own dream. He would have been justified to move on to the next cell and forget the sadness of the men. He didn't have to linger with them. But he was a leader. And he lived for others not himself.

So he said to them, "Tell me your dreams." Wow! What a profound statement. It not only confirmed a healing in Joseph's own soul but it highlighted the secret to his leadership success. He was a releaser of dreams. He cared about the dreams of others and he sought to aid in their fulfillment.

He practiced this without favoritism. He sought to fulfill the dreams of his leaders and he sought to serve the dreams of those under him. This selfless exercise of love became his salvation. When he paused beside the cell of two sad prisoners he had no way of knowing that some day Pharaoh would have a dream of his own. He had no idea that his practice of blessing the dreams of others would launch him to the throne.

Do you remember how it happened? Pharaoh dreamed a dream that no one could interpret. Except Joseph. Literally overnight, Joseph went from being the right-hand man of the prison warden to the right-hand man of the king. He said to Pharaoh, "Tell me your dreams," and his career was launched. It took a decade of testing and trials but his hour had come. He was promoted to the second-most powerful position in the kingdom.

Wherever he went, men ran before his chariot commanding the people to bow their knees before him. He had prestige, wealth, and fame. And God was with him.

He is the perfect picture of marketplace ministry. He's the perfect picture of moral purity. He's the perfect picture of how practicing encouragement and selfless service of the dreams of others opens the door to prosperity and promotion.

"I have dreamed a dream!" Have you? Don't ever give up on it! Think about this—if *your* dream comes true, *God's* Kingdom gets advanced in the earth. He needs you. Some sad man in the adjacent office needs you. Pharaoh needs you.

It's amazing that at the end of Joseph's story he could see the hand of God in all that had transpired. He was married. He had two sons, Manasseh and Ephraim. The names of his sons meant *forgetting* and *fruitfulness.* He said that God had made him forget all of his toil and had made him fruitful in the land of his affliction. He was rich. He was respected. Pharaoh, just like Potiphar and the prison warden, didn't bother to concern himself with anything under Joseph's charge. What a testimony for a right-hand man!

Possibly the most remarkable testimony to Joseph's life came when he was finally reunited with his brothers in Egypt. He said to them, "God has made me a father to Pharaoh." The Lord used Joseph—the young, dreaming prisoner—to become a spiritual father to the most powerful man in the world.

Here are the secrets to his success:

1. The Lord was with him.

2. He never relinquished his moral purity.

3. His faithful service won the hearts of his leaders.

4. He was selfless enough, despite his own pain, to notice sad eyes in the cell beside him.

5. He was a releaser of the dreams of others.

As an associate leader, your success hinges on your ability to do the same. Cling to Jesus. Stay pure. Serve. Have eyes to see into the souls of those around you. Become an identifier and releaser of dreams. Someday you, too, will say of your trials, "God meant it for good."

Tell me your dreams!

Men make history, and not the other way around. In periods where there is no leadership, society stands still. Progress occurs when courageous, skillful leaders seize the opportunity to change things for the better.

-Harry S. Truman

Leadership is the challenge to be something more than average.

-Jim Rohn

Do not go where the path may lead, go instead where there is no path and leave a trail.

-Ralph Waldo Emerson

THE FINGERPRINT OF GOD

Creation was speechless that day. They watched in fascinated awe as their Creator donned a potter's robe. Although His glory was slightly veiled beneath this cloak, He still over-shadowed the splendor of Eden. The infant wonders of earth diminished around Him as He took His seat beside the potter's wheel.

Creation could look at Him today. They could see the expression of His eyes.

It was love.

The wheel turned as He began to press and mold the clay. Dust and water merged as, before their eyes, the most spectacular of beings took shape and likeness. He was like God—but sleeping.

The smile in the Creator's eyes touched His lips as He bent over the lifeless being on the wheel and breathed His very nature into his soul. The man leapt to his feet and saw, in his first experience of sight, the beauty of his maker. He leapt from the wheel into the outstretched arms of Eternity.

God and man, Creator and image-bearer, Father and son turned and walked away from creation into the splendor of Eden.

They were holding hands as they departed for the first of their many evening walks, and as their backsides came into the view of creation, all of Heaven and earth gasped, for the man, in addition to carrying the breath of the Creator in his lungs, was marked with *the very fingerprint of God.*

◆◆◆◆◆

It's a true story, you know. God formed Adam out of the dust of the earth. The word *formed* describes a lump of clay that is squeezed into shape on the potter's wheel. One of the most wondrous consequences of being formed by the hand of God is that God's fingerprints cover His handiwork. Adam bore the imprint of the hand of God.

So do you.

A major key to enjoying your calling and obtaining security in it is to understand that you are carrying the fingerprint of God on your life.

Do you know much about fingerprints? We probably all know the basics.

Our fingerprints do not change throughout our lifetime. The fingerprint of a grandfather is unchanged from the day of his birth. The same is true of the call of God. It remains unchanged throughout our lifetimes. The plan that He has for us is unalterable. It is secure.

Our fingerprints are uniquely different from any other set of prints on the planet. Out of the billions and billions of sets of fingerprints available today, yours are unique. No one has your mark. When fingerprinting was becoming a serious arena of study, they began testing identical twins to see if it was possible that two people could have the same set of prints. Many thousands of twins were tested and never once has a set of twins had the same fingerprints.

Our fingerprints authenticate our identity. Isn't that the heart cry of every person? Mankind is in a search for the authentication of their identity. Fingerprints authenticate identity in two ways. They answer the questions:

1. *Who is this person?* Fingerprints can verify identity when there is either no claim of identity made or when there is a multitude of possibilities for identity.

2. *Is this person who they claim to be?* Once an assertion of identity is made, fingerprints can affirm the claim.

The fingerprints of God on our lives accomplish the same things. Amidst a search for identity among the endless possibilities offered by the world, His mark identifies who we are. Once we begin to walk in our identity as His sons and daughters, His mark on our nature affirms that, yes, this is indeed who we are.

It's interesting to me that the television show *C.S.I.* (a television program that explores the science of forensics in criminal investigations) has become so popular among this generation. I wonder if it's a prophetic sign that this generation is seeking for its origins.

Jesus addressed this search. Do you remember when He was challenged by some of His critics about the obligation to pay taxes? They were seeking to trip Him up in His speech and find something to use against Him. He turned the tables on them, however, and addressed a completely different, more fundamental, issue. He said, "Bring Me a coin." When He held the coin in His hand, He asked, "Whose likeness is stamped on the coin?" When they rightly replied, "Caesar's," Jesus said, "Then give to Caesar the things that are Caesar's...." They were okay with that response. What bothered them was His next statement: "...and give to God the things that are God's."

It confused them because it didn't seem to have anything to do with paying taxes. They were right. Jesus was asking the deepest of all questions. He asked, *"Whose likeness is stamped on you?"* He was basically saying, *"You belong to the Father. Therefore give to God the things that are God's."* Jesus was addressing His life mission to seek and save the lost. He said, "The identity that you are seeking is found only in the Father. It's *His* likeness that is stamped on the center of your nature. To find yourself you must run to Him."

How does all of this pertain to leadership? It's very simple. Since you bear the mark of God that no one else on the planet has, there is an aspect of His nature that only you can display to His creation. The world needs your unique leadership!

A major pitfall for leaders is the temptation of comparison with other leaders. None of us are exempt from it. We have to master it, however, because it is deadly.

I need to confess to you that I recently became ensnared by this temptation. My daily drive to my daughter's school takes me past a church that is more than five times the size of my congregation, and as I viewed its campus I began to grow discontent.

I had no desire to leave my church; I just wanted it to grow more quickly. I began to feel like I was missing the mark in my leadership. By comparing myself to others, I was falling prey to something demonic. I had forgotten that the Lord does not deal with us through comparison with others—the enemy does.

There are only two standards by which we will be judged. We will be judged by the standard of Jesus Christ as found in the Word of God and we will be judged by the call of God on our lives. When we stand before God someday, He will not ask us why we weren't more like our colleagues or competitors. He will ask, "Why weren't you more like Jesus? And why weren't you more like *you*?"

The world needs me. And it needs you. It doesn't matter how greatly the Lord uses your senior leader. It doesn't matter how many employees the business down the street houses. It doesn't matter how big the congregation across town is. We are called for a specific purpose, and it is *only* found in the center of His will.

When I recognized that I had become snared by the enemy and my own pride, I had to repent. I built an altar in my heart and I surrendered my will to Him again. I wrote in my journal:

"I want Your will; nothing more nothing less. I want to fulfill every nuance of Your plan for me. My goal in life is not to pastor a church of 10,000-my goal is to fulfill Your purpose for my life in my generation. Help me to discern Your will. Help me to know Your plan for me. Help me

to please You. If You have called me to pastor a church of 10,000 people, I won't settle for anything less than 10,000. If You have called me to pastor a church of 500, let me pastor it with such incredible excellence that it pleases You and impresses Heaven. Lord, I submit to You again. I surrender my agenda and ambition. Help me to faithfully maximize every stage of my training along the way. I don't want to skip a single lesson. I don't want to bypass any grades. Train me thoroughly. Teach me all that I need to know. Help me to maximize the potential of every season of life.

"I re-devote myself to the priority of Your presence. Forgive me for burning wick instead of oil. Forgive me for feeding and leading Your people from my own soul. I am so sorry! I run back to prayer. I reconstruct my life on the foundation of Your presence and Your Word. I build an altar at this juncture of my life and I offer You my will."

I met Him that day! Grace returned to me. I fell in love with leadership again.

Leading is wonderful when it's done in accordance with the fingerprint of God on your life. David said, "My lot is secure." You need to know that your portion is secure. No one can take it away. No one else's skill in leadership can nullify your role to play.

I said at the start of this book that you are worth your weight in gold. I hope you believe me. Your Father certainly does. You bear His imprint. He trusted you enough to put His nature in you. There's no other leader like you. You're priceless. Carry on!

Since Paul had high hopes for Timothy, he set about to correct Timothy's timid nature, to replace softness with steel. Paul led Timothy into experiences and hardships that toughened his character. Paul did not hesitate to assign him tasks beyond his present powers. How else can a young person develop competence and confidence if not by stretching to the impossible?

-J. Oswald Sanders

Jigoro Kano was the founder of the martial art of judo. His story is a lesson of inspiration and motivation for every student of life.

Kano possessed an extraordinary willingness to learn. He sought out the nearly defunct martial art of jujitsu and modified it to incorporate modern sports principles, creating the art of judo. It became the defense system of the Japanese police and was the first Eastern martial art to be accepted in international competition at the Olympics.

Kano was so focused on learning new and improved techniques in all walks of life that he found new and better ways for the island nation of Japan to educate its youth. He became known as the father of modern Japanese education. Kano was well respected in athletic, social, and political circles worldwide.

Just before he died, this world-renowned martial arts expert called his students together. As they congregated to hear the final words of their judo master, he announced, "When you bury me, do not bury me in a black belt! Be sure to bury me in a white belt."

In martial arts the white belt is the symbol of a beginner—an apprentice who has many things yet to learn.

What a lesson in humility and teachability! Each of us, regardless of our ranking in life, must become a lifelong learner.

-Wayne Cordeiro

chapter fifteen

THE NEXT GENERATION LEADER

There comes a day when some associate leaders succeed their predecessors. Done appropriately, this can be a glorious event. If senior leaders and their right-hand men can walk out the generational transfer of leadership successfully, and without rushing the process, we will have an army of qualified leaders emerge in the 21st century.

Premature promotion often results in disaster while overly delayed promotion often results in frustration and a breach in relationship. When the timing is right, however, relationships between the senior and associate leaders remain strong, the people rejoice, and the Kingdom of God is advanced.

One of the best outlines for a successful transition of leadership can be seen in the relationship between King David and his son.

King Solomon: He was the wisest man of all time. He was famous for his wealth and splendor and for the proverbs that poured from his lips. Most of us know some of the details of his life, but did you know that he was anointed as king *twice*? Did you know that he served as a right-hand man for a long time before he was released to lead on his own?

A careful study of the transition of leadership between Solomon and his father, David, shows that they walked through eight distinct stages of growth and development before there was a complete transition of the leadership reins. Here are those stages:

1. David identified Solomon as his successor.

2. David charged Solomon with the vision (building a house for the Lord).

3. David trained Solomon.

4. David set Solomon in as king. (This was his first anointing as king.)

5. David continued to do the bulk of the leading (while Solomon was king).

6. David set Solomon in fully as king. (This was his second anointing as king.)

7. David transitioned the support of his key leaders to Solomon.

8. David died and Solomon reigned in his stead.

Can you see where you are in this process with your senior leader? Have you ever clearly identified the process of transition and its required stages of growth and development? It's very eye-opening to realize that the transition generally takes longer than we might realize. Sure, the reins of leadership can be transferred overnight, but for the highest assurance of success these eight steps must be taken.

1. David identified Solomon as his successor.

This is a great day in the life of a young leader. Unfortunately, there is usually quite a gap in time between the identification and the release. David was anointed king at Bethlehem as a ruddy, young sheep-herder but he didn't ascend the throne until a decade later. Paul was commissioned as a chosen vessel from the Lord and then went into relative obscurity for 13 years.

2. David charged Solomon with the vision.

It takes time to crystallize the calling and the vision. The call of God can be a very generic thing until maturity and the dealings of the Lord bring it into focus. Although some people receive a clearly defined vision at the time of their calling from the Lord, others simply receive a general sense of being set apart for a great purpose.

I've heard many young Bible college students tell me that they are called to the ministry, but they didn't have a clue which specific aspect of the ministry they were called to. Often, it's not until we have lived through certain experiences and have allowed the Lord to shape our hearts and minds that we are able to perceive the specifics of our calling.

I was visiting with a young man the other night after a worship service, and he was telling me how inspired he was to break into the world of real estate investing. Never mind that he had no money and hadn't read a single book on business or real estate. He just knew that God was calling him "into business." It's usually like that. The calling descends upon our life and then we are enrolled in the Holy Spirit's school of preparation and training.

What God had commissioned Solomon to build was bigger than the work of a mere man. It was a God-sized work, and David was careful to ensure that Solomon understood the vision completely.

3. David trained Solomon.

The training that future leaders require is intense. It's not merely an academic education that young leaders need but it is training in maturity, philosophy of thinking, conflict resolution, leadership, and relational skills. They must be able to articulate and communicate vision well. They must be skilled in relating with people of varying backgrounds and life situations.

Think of the requirements for leaders that Paul passed on to Timothy. As Timothy was installing leaders in the church, he was supposed to look for men of moral purity, rock solid character, healthy families, strong communication skills, and the ability to relate well with people. These traits do not develop overnight.

It's a surprise to many young leaders when they are identified as future kings and then they are sentenced to the backside of the desert instead of the throne. They often think they're ready. The degree on their office wall confirms it.

I had a couple of degrees and several years of experience before I entered my current position of leadership. Even so, I wasn't nearly prepared enough for all that the Lord would require of me. I thought I was. My six years in Bible college helped to prepare me. My five years in a paid ministry position helped to prepare me. My years in business prepared me (in many ways I learned far more about leadership and ministry through my business experience than I did in Bible school). What I have realized, though, is that most of my learning (in all of my leadership roles) has been on the job.

Pioneers can't fully prepare in advance. Any time you attempt to launch a new business or begin a new work there will be numerous aspects to it that you can only learn as you get into it. Ongoing mentoring, then, becomes a crucial component of leadership development.

4. David set Solomon in as king (his *first* anointing).

This would possibly be equivalent to being installed as the second-in-command leader. Although there was a measure of authority granted, there was still a very hands-on senior leader around to provide the bulk of the leadership and direction.

A quick pointer for young Solomons who are in this position is to embrace every opportunity to handle the tough leadership issues. One of the fastest ways for a young leader to grow is to make a firm commitment to never shirk the tough decisions and situations that a senior leader must face. One day you'll *have* to face them—you'll be the top leader. Today, you can still defer to your senior leader; however, if you would make it a practice to embrace every opportunity to grow, you will be miles ahead in your development. Tough issues must be confronted. Delicate conversations must be engaged in. Wisdom would tell you to do it now while your senior leader is available to mentor you.

Let me share a quick thought regarding mentoring. I believe that the degree of mentoring that is received is contingent on the degree of desire and tenacity in the one being mentored. It's impossible to mentor someone who doesn't want it. When someone desires to grow, however, they can be mentored in any situation regardless of the skills or weaknesses of the parties involved.

I work with a young man who is destined to be a senior leader. Incredibly sharp, he could wonderfully run his department with little or no oversight from me. However, he hungers to be mentored so he seizes every possible opportunity to ask me questions. He asks the right questions. He doesn't just ask me what the right thing is to *do*. He asks me *how to do it* and *why it should be done that way*. He wants to get inside the head of every leader he knows so he can glean from both the good and the bad.

I have learned a mentoring principle that has helped me tremendously in my relationship with my senior leader. Asking the right questions will help your leader mentor you. If I sit down with my leader and ask, "Will you mentor me?" He will want to know specifics. What do I want? What am I looking for?

I constantly ask him why he handles situations the way he does. I want to know why certain things bother him while others don't seem to faze him at all. I want inside his head and I want inside his heart.

Proverbs 20:5 says, "*The purposes of a man's heart are deep waters, but a man of understanding draws them out*" (NIV). Draw them out of your leader.

5. David continued to do the bulk of the leading (even though Solomon had been anointed as king).

It can be a challenge for young leaders when they feel that they are ready to lead on their own (and they may be) and yet they are not fully empowered to do so. For leaders in this situation, I think that the best mind-set they can adopt is that of a student. Determine that you will glean every possible lesson from your current situation. Until the day comes that the reins are transitioned fully to you, do your best to learn and grow. Master your leadership skills. Become the expert on your specific niche of leadership responsibility.

Do you remember Amos? He spent his lifetime in preparation and was called to center stage for only a very brief period of time. He delivered his prophetic message and preached the word for a few months and then went back to tending sheep. Make the most of your preparation.

While you're at it, have fun.

Enjoy your role as second in command. You are a highly trusted and respected leader. Enjoy it! Enjoy the fact that you walk in authority but you still have a senior leader around to help carry the weight of the organization with you. Someday the buck will stop with you so enjoy the fact that you still have his help and support.

6. David set Solomon fully in as king (his second anointing as king).

Did you notice that at each stage *David* did the setting? Self-appointed and self-promoted leaders are short-lived leaders. Solomon had a brother named Adonijah who declared himself king. His reign was never fully recognized and it only lasted for a few hours.

The only way to ensure longevity in leadership is to allow *the Lord* to promote you in *His* timing. The Book of Daniel tells a story of young leaders who maximized the time of their preparation, trusted the Lord, and then enjoyed a lifetime of promotion in government. It's a story for *you*.

7. David transitioned the support of his key leaders to Solomon.

David said to his key leaders (after all of these stages of development and transition were complete), "Solomon, my son, is *still* young and inexperienced." Despite all of the training and preparation, Solomon still needed the wisdom of his elders to guide him. The strongest leadership is that which has a multi-generational element.

One of the most profound Scriptures that illustrates this leadership principle is found in Second Chronicles 10:7. Rehoboam was king. His father, Solomon, had died and transitioned the kingdom to him. The citizens of the kingdom had grown restless and impatient with some of the heavy taxation of Solomon's reign. They appealed to him to show mercy and to lead the nation in a new and fresh direction. Wisely, Rehoboam sought counsel from the elders, his father's friends and advisors, and they offered some of the best advice that a young, emerging leader can receive. They said, "If you will be a servant to these people and will speak kindly to them, then they will be your servants forever."

Before acting upon their advice, however, Rehoboam decided to counsel with *his* friends. They were young, untested, and unseasoned leaders who said, "You should tell them that if they thought your father was bad, you will be worse. Say 'he chastised you with whips, but I will chastise you with scorpions.'"

Sadly, Rehoboam listened to their counsel and he became one of the worst leaders in Israel's history.

Seek wise counsel. Surround yourself with the right kind of counselors. Gather people who understand and own the vision, who truly love and believe in you, and who are not afraid to speak truth to you.

8. David died and Solomon reigned in his stead.

John Maxwell is famous for saying, "Everything rises and falls on leadership." I think that for the welfare of future generations it is safe to also say, "Everything rises and falls on the successful transition of leadership."

In the following pages, my senior leader, Dutch Sheets, shares some practical wisdom regarding mentoring young leaders that will help to ensure that the transition is a success.

The growth and development of people is the highest calling of leadership.

-Harvey S. Firestone

Teaching is a continuous cycle of teaching, inquiry into practice, self-assessment, self-prescription, and re-teaching.

-Ellen Moir

Nearly all men can stand adversity, but if you want to test a man's character give him power.

-Abraham Lincoln

MENTORING THE NEXT GENERATION LEADER— PART I (DUTCH SHEETS)

Chris has done a great job of providing insight for those who serve in the role of second in command. He embodies what he has shared and is truly a faithful son in the Lord. Although it would be premature to declare that we have successfully completed our journey, if the future is as successful as the past, in the end it will have been a great success.

My aim, in this chapter and the next, is to share some general principles for the man or woman at the top in a relationship such as ours. I'm certainly not saying that if you're the second in command you won't glean valuable information from these insights—you will—but, nonetheless, they are intended more for the leader. I have 12 of them, six of which I will share here in this chapter, with the final six in the next chapter.

Principle Number 1

Make sure the person you're training has your heart and spiritual DNA. I know this seems rather basic, but believe me, it isn't. I have wasted a lot of time in the past trying to father hirelings who didn't really want to connect with my heart, passion, and vision. They wanted various things—jobs, stepping stones to future ministry, even mentoring—but they weren't likeminded enough to be long-term. And since they didn't connect at a heart level, they had difficulty accepting discipline or correction, weren't terribly loyal, and again, didn't stay very long. Don't waste your time investing in relationships such as these. Chris, on the other hand, has my spiritual DNA, and has connected with me at a heart level. It is easy, therefore, to build together and very easy for me to trust him, and vice versa.

I heard a wise elder say to young men once that when seeking God's will for their lives, they should not start by asking "where," but "with whom." Nothing could be truer. His point was to start with relationship. We, as leaders, must think in the same way, asking the question, "Who is God joining me with at a heart level, in order that I might build a lasting and fruitful relationship with them?" We want a *marriage*, not an *affair*.

Principle Number 2

Make sure the person you are training already considers you a spiritual father or mother to them, or at the very least understands and desires such a relationship. This is the next logical issue after number one. God is moving the church away from old and unbiblical paradigms that cause us to operate and look more like secular corporations than like family. He is moving us toward covenantal relationships that mirror biblical models offered by Paul and Timothy, Elijah and Elisha, Moses and Joshua and others. These relationships involved fathers and sons, not just mentors and students.

Paul didn't say to the Corinthian church, "you have not many mentors," nor did he use the term "bosses" (see 1 Cor. 4:15). He used the term "*father*" to describe the relationship. I'm not looking for someone to mentor; I'm looking for someone to father. Children can receive information and knowledge from teachers or mentors, but they receive their identity, security, character, and core values from parents.

Both the Charismatic and Jesus Movements of the 60s and 70s were greatly used of God, but neither lived up to its full potential, largely because they spawned many young leaders who were not discipled and trained by mothers and fathers in the faith. Consequently, these young leaders were both dysfunctional and immature. In fact, I cannot imagine a movement in church history that placed so many novices in leadership positions. The results were devastating:

- Leaders who produced action without accountability.

- *Works*-oriented ministries that didn't know the ways of God.

- Dominating, lording, and independent-minded leaders (because they hadn't learned to lead by serving).

- Leaders who prostituted their gifts for gain and spawned a generation of "what's-in-it-for-me" Christians.

- A theologically shallow Body of Christ, which became easy prey to deception and superficial belief systems.

- Leaders who knew how to birth spiritual children, but not how to train and nurture daughters and sons.

We have been on a 20-year (or so) course correction. God is joining the generations. As He does, what will true spiritual father and mother relationships do for the sons and daughters?

- Seeing the subtleties of pride and selfish ambition, we will teach them humility.

- Recognizing the danger of isolation and one-person shows, we will teach dependence—our need for one another.

- Understanding the seasons of the Spirit, we will teach patience—the ability to wait.

- Knowing one can't build on miracles, sensation, and the *works* of God, we will teach the *ways* of God and the principles of His Word.

- Knowing the strength and subtlety of sin, we will demonstrate the need for and provide accountability.

- Helping sons and daughters become fathers and mothers, we will prevent the next generation from being spiritually illegitimate.

- The connection with us will remove the curse from the land (see Mal. 4:6).

Chris is a spiritual son to me; I'm a father to him. Because of this, I am passing on more than knowledge and how-to's—I am giving life. And because he has a spiritual father, he will one day be one. Together, we are making certain that the bastard spirit does not enter our spiritual house, and that the security of family is being reproduced.

Principle Number 3

When parenting spiritual sons and daughters, don't try to clone yourself. Reproduce, yes. Multiply yourself, absolutely. But when physical parents multiply themselves, their children are like them, but still unique. They have similar DNA, mind-sets, and personalities, and may even resemble the parents physically, but they will not be clones. Likewise, our spiritual children will resemble us in many ways, but also be unique. If impartation occurs while still leaving room for diversity, our spiritual sons and daughters will go far beyond us in their accomplishments.

Elisha was like Elijah, and yet different. Joshua gleaned much from Moses, but led with his own unique gifts and strengths. So too, we must shape without cookie-cutting, mold without stereotyping. I try to allow Chris's uniqueness to be released. I allow and encourage him to do some things *his* way, not *mine*. I even allow and encourage certain facets of the church to look like him, rather than me. This causes growth in Chris, and actually makes the church stronger.

Principle Number 4

Allow those in training to fall short once in a while. Like any wise biological parent with their child, I allow and actually want Chris to learn some things by messing up—I just don't want big messes. I have actually allowed him to do some things his way, all the while knowing they weren't the best way. Why? There are several reasons:

- I wanted him to know he wasn't ready for certain responsibilities. Most of us at times think we are farther along in our development than we really are. If I had simply told Chris his limitation, he may not have accepted it. Experiencing it left no doubt.

- I wanted the humility that failure would create. It's not that Chris has pride issues, at least no more than the rest of us; it's just that humility is such a strength that I want him to walk in a high—or should I say low?—level of it.

- I wanted him to have to clean up after the wrong decision. This would also be valuable training, teaching him responsibility and problem-solving.

- I wanted Chris to know his acceptance is not predicated on perfection. I told him early on, "This is a safe place to make mistakes." I demand loyalty, integrity, faithfulness, and other virtues but never perfection. I want those under me to know they are accepted and loved, even when they are less than perfect. This will allow them to make difficult decisions later on without fearing failure. This is how our heavenly Father deals with us; we should do no less.

Principle Number 5

Work on heart and character issues as much or more than you do how-to's and gift development. Obviously, Chris already receives high marks in character and purity of heart. But in all of us there are weak areas of our hearts that can go undetected. David knew this and asked God to show him any weaknesses there (see Ps. 139:23-24).

Many casualties have occurred among church leaders because they were allowed to rise to their position based on the strength of their gifts and innovative abilities. Character took a back seat. This has many pitfalls, some of which include:

- Building on hype and sensation versus substance and depth.

- Pride, which in turn produces an independent spirit, a spirit of control, an inability to properly receive praise, building a kingdom for self, and a host of other bad things.

- Performance mind-sets.

- A competitive spirit.

- Prioritizing innovation over the anointing and seeking of God.

- Allowing instant gratification to replace long-term building.

- Zeal trumping wisdom.

- Vision born of ambition rather than God's heart.

Asahel, one of King David's young soldiers, was a prime example of this. Though he was very gifted and on the right side, he was killed by an older and wiser soldier. Here is the account:

> *Now the three sons of Zeruiah were there, Joab and Abishai and Asahel; and Asahel was as swift-footed as one of the gazelles which is in the field. And Asahel pursued Abner and did not turn to the right or to the left from following Abner. Then Abner looked behind him and said, "Is that you, Asahel?" And he answered, "It is I." So Abner said to him, "Turn to your right or to your left, and take hold of one of the young men for yourself, and take for yourself his spoil." But Asahel was not willing to turn aside from following him. And Abner repeated again to Asahel, "Turn aside from following me. Why should I strike you to the ground? How then could I lift up my face to your brother Joab?" However, he refused to turn aside; therefore Abner struck him in the belly with the butt end of the spear, so that the spear came out at his back. And he fell there and died on the spot. And it came about that all who came to the place where Asahel had fallen and died, stood still"* (2 Samuel 2:18-23).

Asahel didn't need more speed or gifting; he needed more seasoning. Though he was younger and faster (giftedness) than Abner, it wasn't enough. Neither was his zeal. I don't want sons and daughters of mine to perish like Asahel. I want them to have long and healthy careers. I desire for them to be people "after God's heart" whose marriages endure, whose children honor them and God, and who build stable and long-lasting ministries. So I prioritize the building of character over gifting.

Principle Number 6

Though similar to the last one, this principle is different. *When training leaders for influential positions, we must prioritize wisdom over knowledge.* I want Chris to one day step into a senior leadership position with more than a lot of head knowledge and how-to's. I want him to have, "a spirit of wisdom and understanding, the spirit of counsel" (Isa. 11:2). Knowledge is the gaining of information; wisdom is the proper application.

Job 11:5-6 says, "Would that God might speak...and show you the secrets of wisdom!" Facts and knowledge can be interpreted in so many ways. That is why judges can disagree over the same set of facts, as can jurists, politicians, religious leaders, and teachers. But "wisdom is the principle thing" (Prov. 4:7 NKJV) and will bring the correct interpretation of the facts. This passage in Proverbs goes on to say in the New American Standard Bible, "Acquire wisdom; and with all your acquiring, get understanding. Prize her, and she will exalt you; she will honor you if you embrace her. She will place on your head a garland of grace; she will present you with a crown of beauty" (Prov. 4:7-9).

Because of this principle, I process a lot with Chris. We talk not only about "what" but "why." I bring him into the decision-making process. I let him watch me in awkward situations, disciplinary matters, and challenging meetings. I want him to know *why* I react and do as I do...to learn the *process* of decision-making, not formulas. I'm trying to build a *man*, not a *machine*.

In Conclusion

As spiritual mothers and fathers in the faith, much of the strength of the church *tomorrow* depends on us *today*. I want to put qualities in tomorrow's leaders that will cause the Church to prosper and move forward when it's their turn to be in charge. I want one day to leave a legacy of sons and daughters who have taken the torch and run well, keeping the flame bright and advancing it well.

Judges 2:10 says, "All that generation also were gathered to their fathers; and there arose another generation after them who did not know the Lord, nor yet the work which He had done for Israel." What a tragedy! I don't want a generation to arise that doesn't know the Lord and His ways. I want God-seekers, God-knowers, and God-pleasers. And that is possible. As we apply these and other principles, we can ensure not only the success of our offspring, but also prosperity of our cause.

The art of being wise is knowing what to overlook.

-William James

The spirited horse, which will try to win the race of its own accord, will run even faster if encouraged.

-Publius Ovidius Naso Ovid

Success consists of going from failure to failure without loss of enthusiasm.

-Sir Winston Leonard Spencer Churchill

Lift, lead, and love.

-Spencer W. Kimball

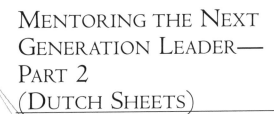

MENTORING THE NEXT GENERATION LEADER— PART 2 (DUTCH SHEETS)

As we in positions of mothering and fathering sow into those coming behind us, there are certain things we must remember. I shared six of them in the last chapter, and will include six more here, making a total of 12.

Principle Number 7

Allow leaders in training to question your methods and ideas and even to disagree with you. I want obedience from those under me, but I don't want blind obedience. Chris doesn't question my authority, but he knows he can question my ideas and that there won't be a relational problem if he disagrees with them. I'm helping to shape him into a wise leader and, as such, I need him to think, not just parrot my thoughts and ideas.

Of course we don't disagree often, but when we do he knows he is free to speak up and say, "I'm not sure that's the best way," or something similar. And sometimes he is right. Even if he is wrong, however, it gives us the opportunity to process so he knows why I'm doing what I do. It also serves to demonstrate to him that his ideas matter—that he is valuable. He knows we're a team, not just a corporation.

Sometimes Chris questions me just to learn. "Why did you handle that the way you did?" is not an unusual thing to hear from him. Or, "Why didn't you do that differently?" Each situation becomes a learning time, as long as he knows he can ask.

Recently, Chris and my wife, Ceci, helped me to see that an aspect of my leadership style needs to change. Each did it independently and unaware of the other. I'm human enough that I don't like hearing about my weaknesses, but more importantly I want to be a good leader. And we can all improve. One of the marks of a secure leader is the ability to acknowledge imperfections, and I want to model that kind of humility for those I lead.

Principle Number 8

I know it seems simple and is a no-brainer in any relationship, but it needs to be said anyway: *over communicate*. This is very challenging for me and my staff because of my call to the nation and the resulting travel. Frankly, it is something that I could have done much better at times and I am trying to improve. But there is no good excuse for poor communication. You can succeed or fail on this point alone.

Never assume that the person under you knows what you want—tell them. I don't particularly like meetings but I realize they are necessary. Chris and I meet over coffee, lunches, and at the office. When I'm at home or on the road, he knows he has the freedom to call me anytime. He doesn't do so often, but he knows he can and sometimes does. He is doing his best to represent me, my heart, and my wishes, and I don't want him to be frustrated trying to figure out what that is. Still, there have been times when I have held up progress and frustrated him or my staff because I have delayed getting answers to them. This is not good leadership.

Another area of communication I frequently try to do with Chris has to do with coaching him. Very often I ask him in a service, "What are you sensing?" or "What do you feel we should do now?" I then give him my thoughts. Our services are not program driven. We make great efforts to release the Holy Spirit to minister in any way

He chooses. This could involve prophecy, laying on hands for healing or other ministry, encouragement, extended worship to draw us closer to the Lord, or various other directions the service could take. It is not always easy to know what to do, and I want Chris to learn how to follow the Spirit's leading now—with a coach beside him. Then when he is the senior leader, he will function with much more wisdom and confidence.

Communicate. Communicate. Communicate.

Principle Number 9

Be real and transparent. Allow those you are training to see your humanness—your weaknesses as well as your strengths, your failures as well as your successes, your disappointments and hurts as well as your excitement.

Jesus allowed the disciples to see His anger when He cleansed the temple, His weariness from ministry, His frustration with unbelief, His indignation toward legalism and religiosity, and His sorrow in the garden. He was secure enough to be real. I try to operate this way with my senior staff and I believe it makes us closer—and it releases them to be real.

Allow your spiritual sons and daughters to see your mistakes. Admit them. Jesus never made any—you will. When you're wrong, say so. When your decision wasn't wise, tell them. Don't spin it; say "I messed up." You are responsible to teach them not only how-to's, but also humility, integrity, and honesty—heart issues.

If they can hear me say I made a mistake, they'll feel free to do the same. They won't be prone toward performance mind-sets, the fear of failure, or other dysfunctional tendencies. I want them to be motivated by truth and what they believe is right—not the fear of failing.

Laugh with them; cry with them; pray with them; play with them. Be real.

Principle Number 10

When training a person to become the senior leader, which is what we believe Chris will one day do, *give them honor with the people.* You have the literal ability to give them favor. God told Moses to "put some of your authority on" Joshua (Num. 27:20). Authority is the Hebrew word *howd,* and means "splendor, majesty, glory, honor, or renown." Moses was told to do this "before all the congregation...in order that all the congregation...may obey him."

Empower those under you to represent you! Give them favor; honor them in front of the people. Transfer some of your "renown" to them. You won't be honored less, just represented more.

Some leaders are afraid for any attention or praise to go to those under them. They think it weakens their ability to be respected and followed. Nothing could be further from the truth. I once heard of an insecure and proud leader who allowed only he and his wife to sit on the front row of chairs on the platform. The rest of the staff had to sit behind them as a picture of submission. The lights on the platform were carefully situated so that a spot was on this man and his wife, in order that they would stand out more than the others.

Two of his staff members were friends of mine, one of them a great youth pastor. My friend had the opportunity to go on radio locally—a person in the congregation wanted to foot the bill. When approached by this youth pastor with the opportunity, the senior pastor's response was, "I'm not on the radio yet. You don't go on the radio until after I get to go on the radio."

What pathetic insecurity. What a dysfunctional leader. He had probably never been fathered spiritually so he couldn't be a spiritual father.

I allow Chris to preach some on Sundays. I have him emcee our services, receive offerings, release those with words of encouragement to share them, allow him to go to the podium and exhort the people without asking my permission, and frequently ask him publicly if he has anything to add at the end of my message and close of the service. I am putting some of my authority on him.

When he steps into the senior role someday, it won't be much of a shock to the people. And it won't be hard for them to honor and follow him because they already do. I am setting him up to succeed later by giving him honor now.

Principle Number 11

In transitioning a spiritual son or daughter into a leading role *don't move too fast or too slow, and don't guess at the timing of their release in advance.* I realize the timing of their ultimate release is very subjective, but it is also extremely important. If you release young leaders too soon, either they will fail or—at the very least—not reach their fullest potential. If you wait too long, hope deferred will set in, bringing with it many potential snares. And if you guess at the timing and it ends up taking longer, again you set the person up for frustration or hope deferred. Walk out the process and trust the Holy Spirit to show you the right time. Here are some things to remember as you do so:

- They will most likely think they are ready before they are. Just as teenagers think they have reached adulthood before they truly have, so it is with spiritual sons and daughters. This is normal. Give them some freedom of expression but don't fully release them until *you* know they are ready.

- You will most likely think they're not ready when they actually are. Again, just like a physical parent, it is hard to let go. There will always be more for younger leaders to learn, but if you don't release them when it's time, you will either create rebellion or stunt their growth. Besides, if you have done your job well, they will want to stay connected and you can still help them.

- One final thing to remember when judging the timing of release is that to a degree it will depend on what they are called to do. Chris could be the senior leader of a church our size now. But God is preparing him to do more than pastor a church. He is called to be a leader of leaders and one day oversee a base of ministry that is much more than just a church. Therefore, God is requiring more from him in the way of training.

Principle Number 12

Insist that the spiritual daughter or son is whole spiritually and emotionally before you release them. This is critical. If you don't, you are guaranteeing their failure, the wounding of others, and a detriment to the cause of Christ. The Body of Christ is full of insecure, controlling, selfish, and arrogant leaders. And since we reproduce after our kind...well, you get the point. If a senior leader is not whole inwardly, several bad things will happen:

- They will respond inappropriately to criticism.

- Their ministry will be to meet a need in them rather than to serve God and honor Him. This is very subtle and often goes undetected, but is prevalent in the Body of Christ.

- They will be performance-oriented and therefore vulnerable to the fear of man, carnal desires to impress, overwork, and burnout. In Exodus 32, the Israelites sinned against God by fashioning an idol and worshiping it while Moses was up on the mountain. Three thousand of the Israelites were destroyed because of this. The amazing thing is that it happened because of Aaron's fear of man. We know he could have stopped the idolatry because the passage says, "for Aaron had let them get out of control" (Exod. 32:25). Insecure leaders fear people more than God.

- They will be susceptible to pride.

- They will judge success outwardly—by size, numbers, notoriety, etc., rather than by obedience.

- They will emphasize gifts over character.

- They will never raise up true sons and daughters of their own.

- Their vision will be controlled by ambition.

- They will become controlling and manipulative. The disciples didn't want others to minister if they weren't following along with them (see Mark 9:38). Joshua didn't want anyone prophesying if they weren't outside the camp with the 70 (see Num. 11:28). These are signs of immaturity. Healthy people share authority and release others.

True spiritual fathers and mothers don't need control but love to see others released into effective ministry.

Join the Generations

God is raising up a generation of believers that will move into leadership positions within the Body of Christ at higher levels of maturity than we have ever seen. It is because of the joining of the generations as described in Malachi 4:6. Do not compromise the process and we will not lose the fruit.

Both the Body of Christ and the cause of Christ in the earth succeed or fail largely based on the strength and maturity of its leaders. The Scriptures demonstrate this time after time. Let's make sure that in our day we reproduce leaders who will one day take the baton smoothly, and run the race well.

REFERENCES

1. Maxwell, John, *The 21 Irrefutable Laws of Leadership* (Thomas Nelson, Inc., Nashville, TN, 1998), p.110.

2. Clayborne Carson and Peter Holloran (editors), *A Knock at Midnight* (Warner Books, Inc., New York, NY, 1998), p. 125.

3. Cordeiro, Wayne, *Attitudes That Attract Success* (Regal Books, Ventura, CA, 2001), pp. 62, 137, 13-14.

4. Sanders, J. Oswald, *Spiritual Leadership* (The Moody Bible Institute, Chicago, IL, 1967, 1980, 1994), pp.27, 79, 144, 148-149.

5. Edwards, Gene, *A Tale of Three Kings* (Tyndale House Publishers, Inc., Wheaton, IL, 1980, 1992), pp. 27-28.

6. Sheets, Dutch, *River of God* (Regal Books, Ventura, CA, 1998), pp. 144-145. Adapted.

7. Zodhiates, Spiros *Hebrew-Greek Key Word Study Bible, New American Standard Bible* (AMG Publishers, Chattanooga, TN, 1977), p. 1721.

8. Roosevelt, Theodore, Citizenship in a Republic Speech, April 23, 1910, Sorbonne Paris. www.theodoreroosevelt.org/life/quotes.htm.

Contact Information

To contact Chris Jackson call
Spring Harvest Fellowship at 719-548-8226.

To contact Dutch Sheets Ministries
Phone: 719-548-8226
Fax: 717-548-8209
Email:
Ministryinfo@dutchsheets.org
Or
www.dutchsheets.org

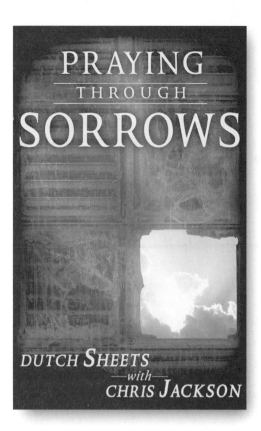

PRAYING THROUGH SORROWS

Doubts, depression and discouragement are characteristic
responses of someone who has endured an experience of "bad
things happening to good people." When a promise from God
does not come to pass, the aftermath is often confusion about
validity of a personal relationship with the Lord. In *Praying Through
Sorrows*, co-authors Dutch Sheets and Chris Jackson confront the
emotional anguish awaiting the arrival of a long delayed break-
through. Forsaking the cliché about the patience of Job, *Praying
Through Sorrows* shows how one overcomes the debilitating state of
"hope deferred making the heart sick," while seeking a restoration
of faith in God's goodness

ISBN 0-7684-2254-X

Available at your local Christian Bookstore.

Additional copies of this book and other
book titles from DESTINY IMAGE are
available at your local bookstore.

For a complete list of our titles,
visit us at www.destinyimage.com
Send a request for a catalog to:

Destiny Image® Publishers, Inc.
P.O. Box 310
Shippensburg, PA 17257-0310

*"Speaking to the Purposes of God for This
Generation and for the Generations to Come"*